The Role of Science in Law

The Role of Science in Law

Robin Feldman

OXFORD
UNIVERSITY PRESS

OXFORD
UNIVERSITY PRESS

Oxford University Press, Inc., publishes works that further Oxford University's objective of excellence in research, scholarship, and education.

Oxford New York
Auckland Cape Town Dar es Salaam Hong Kong Karachi Kuala Lumpur Madrid Melbourne Mexico City Nairobi New Delhi Shanghai Taipei Toronto

With offices in
Argentina Austria Brazil Chile Czech Republic France Greece Guatemala Hungary Italy Japan Poland Portugal Singapore South Korea Switzerland Thailand Turkey Ukraine Vietnam

Published by Oxford University Press, Inc.
198 Madison Avenue, New York, New York 10016

Library of Congress Cataloging-in-Publication Data

Feldman, Robin.
The role of science in law / Robin Feldman.
p. cm.
Includes bibliographical references and index.
ISBN 978-0-19-536858-1 ((hardback) : alk. paper)
1. Science and law--United States. 2. Technological innovations--Law and legislation--United States. I. Title.
KF385.F45 2009
344.73'095--dc22

2008042085

---

1 2 3 4 5 6 7 8 9

Printed in the United States of America on acid-free paper

Note to Readers
This publication is designed to provide accurate and authoritative information in regard to the subject matter covered. It is based upon sources believed to be accurate and reliable and is intended to be current as of the time it was written. It is sold with the understanding that the publisher is not engaged in rendering legal, accounting, or other professional services. If legal advice or other expert assistance is required, the services of a competent professional person should be sought. Also, to confirm that the information has not been affected or changed by recent developments, traditional legal research techniques should be used, including checking primary sources where appropriate.

(Based on the Declaration of Principles jointly adopted by a Committee of the American Bar Association and a Committee of Publishers and Associations.)

This book is dedicated to my husband Boris and our children Natalie, Talya, Eli, Sam, and Adam. It is also dedicated to Professors Bob Weisberg and Gerry Gunther, to whom I will always be grateful for their inspiration

Contents

Acknowledgments

I am grateful to Vik Amar, Margreth Barrett, Richard Epstein, David Faigman, Robert Gordon, David Jung, Sonia Katyal, Donald Kennedy, Greg Kline, Evan Lee, Jeff Lefstin, Mark Lemley, David Levine, Roger Park, Reuel Schiller, Bill Simon, Chris Slobogin, and Lois Weithorn. I am also tremendously grateful to the Chip Robertson Research Fund for support of the project. I wish to thank Cassandra Christiansen, David DeVito, Adam Engelhart, Evgeni Halavanau, Daniel Leroux, Lisa Li, William Mullen, Sudhir Pala, Serena Sanders, Dominic Signorotti, Phong Wu, Brandon Yasnogorodskiy, and Brandon Yu for their research assistance. I am particularly grateful to Mike Dean and James Beard, not only for research assistance but also for coordinating the efforts of the research team. I am indebted beyond measure to Linda Weir, U.C. Hastings Public Services Librarian. I also wish to thank John A. Collins, Lamont Research Services, Harvard University. Finally, I wish to thank participants in the Annual Intellectual Property Scholars' Conference, the Chicago Intellectual Property Colloquium, and the Stanford Program in Law, Science, and Technology for their comments. Earlier versions of selected portions of the book have been published in the following: Historic Perspectives on Law & Science, STANFORD TECH. L. REV. (2008); Law's Misguided Love Affair with Science, MINN. J.L. SCI. & TECH. (2009); Plain Language Patents, 17 TEX. INTELL. PROP. L.J. (2008–2009).

Abstract

The allure of science has always captivated members of the legal profession. Its siren's song offers a tune of perfection and the promise of endowing law with the respect and deference from society that we crave. We continually look to science to rescue us from the discomfort of difficult legal decisions, and we are constantly disappointed.

The powerful allure of science flows in part from our distress over the imperfections of law. With twentieth-century legal theory ringing in our ears, it is tempting to see law as a hopeless enterprise, distorted by biases, hampered by ineptitude, and cluttered with contradictions. Anything deconstructed loses power, although ultimately, the instinct to deconstruct everything loses power, itself, by leaving nothing. Nevertheless, with these critical perspectives in mind, the call of science is particularly strong.

This book traces the interrelation of law and science, analyzing law's attempts to import science into law and attempts to export law's problems to science. Though most authors frame problems at the intersection of law and science in terms of how rapidly scientific information changes and how frequently the legal system distorts science, this book argues that problems at the intersection of law and science flow not from the changing nature of science but from the changing nature of law. With this in mind, the book uses examples from doctrines related to abortion, gene patenting, copyright, environmental regulation, antitrust law, the insanity defense, and other topics to explore the nature of law and to suggest approaches for making science work more effectively within the domain of law. Most important, the book argues that we are unlikely to avoid the cycles of exaltation and disappointment unless we are willing to relinquish the desire for completion and perfection in law.

CHAPTER I

The Allure of Science

The allure of science has always captivated members of the legal profession. Its siren's song has followed us throughout much of American legal history. Science offers a tune of perfection, of elegance, of solid dependability and the promise of endowing law and legal actors with the respect and deference from society that we crave. Most important, we look to science to rescue us from the experience of uncertainty and the discomfort of difficult legal decisions. The notion of what constitutes science and what it would take to make law more scientific varies across time. What does not vary is our constant return to the well. We are constantly seduced into believing that some new science will provide answers to law's dilemmas, and we are constantly disappointed.

Our perpetual forays to find better law through science are incapable of solving law's frustrations, but they do create distortions in the legal realm. When the legal system relies on science to craft its rules, those rules lack the flexibility and dexterity necessary for effective participation in the process of legal evolution. The rules are poorly understood by the legal actors who must apply them, which makes them ill suited to the process of interpretation, evolution, and adaptation essential to the enterprise of law. Instead of engaging in this evolutionary process, we become fixated on scientific categorizations, as if lines drawn by science have some mysterious power that we can access by invoking them.[1]

The history of the law and science interface is replete with examples in which law tries to solve its problems through science and is subsequently disappointed. What is most striking about this pattern is that we repeat it generation after generation in field after field of law with remarkable amnesia about our past failures. My goal in this book is to analyze that pattern and to explore the reasons for its repetition.

As I have worked on this project, I have been constantly reminded of how often the pattern appears, not just across time, but in modern discourse. For example, in 2007, the *New York Times Magazine* featured a long article gushing about how historians of the future will look back on the 1990s as the time when neuroscience began to "transform the American legal system."[2] The article describes new brain scan technology that allows researchers to see what portions of the brain are activated by a particular person in response to a given stimulus. The article describes the great enthusiasm of those who believe that the research will eventually

1 *Cf.* Roscoe Pound, *Mechanical Jurisprudence*, 8 COLUM. L. REV. 605, 606 (1908) (arguing that "[t]he effect of all system is apt to be petrification of the subject systematized. Perfection of scientific system and exposition tends to cut off individual initiative in the future, to stifle independent consideration of new problems and of new phases of old problems, and to impose the ideas of one generation upon another").

2 Jeffrey Rosen, *The Brain on Sand*, N.Y. TIMES, Mar. 11, 2007, *available at* http://www.nytimes.com/2007/03/11/magazine/11Neurolaw.t.html (last accessed Feb. 23, 2008) (on file with author).

allow the legal system to scientifically answer a myriad of troubling questions, including when individuals should *not* be held accountable for their actions and whether a particular individual will engage in future criminal activity. Most important, we are told that the scans will eventually answer the elusive question of just what are our deeply shared beliefs upon which the legal system should be based.

Brain scan imaging and the information it reveals are indeed marvelous. Nevertheless, the excitement over law and neuroscience follows well-worn paths of hope. If only science could give us categories, or something to measure, or if we could find the right configuration of experts, law's problems would dissolve. Before the latest version of "how science will solve law's problems" sweeps us away, it is worth thinking about our past failures in this realm.

This book explores a number of occasions in which law turns to science, sometimes quite explicitly and sometimes with less awareness. The subtle examples are most interesting because they reveal something about how we get into this pattern of reaching for science and why our attempts to solve law's dilemmas in this fashion are so frequently unsuccessful.

The examples reveal a deep-seated dissatisfaction with law's solutions and an instinct to look for definitional frameworks from external sources. We place those frameworks within law and try to use them as doctrinal structures. Of course, doctrinal structures are not enduring. There are no ultimate doctrinal structures in law because there are no ultimate questions. Those wishing to escape the constraints of any doctrinal structure will seek the open spaces, the interstices among those things that have been decided. Cases will naturally emerge within the spaces of whatever structure exists, rendering that structure insufficient for resolving the new question.

Imagine if it were true that every time scientists figured out something about nature, nature tried to change itself.

For example, suppose that when we learned something about how a cell replicates, the cell responded by saying, "Ah, I'd better try another route." If that were true, science would be a very different enterprise. Yet that is the nature of law and the nature of human beings within the legal system.

There is, of course, the famous Heisenberg uncertainty principle in science which holds that in the subatomic realm, observing some features can compromise the ability to observe other features.[3] In other words, in some circumstances, studying a scientific phenomenon without altering it may be difficult. The difficulty of observation without interference in science, however, is quite different from the standard behavior in the legal system in which subjects engage in intentional alteration to avoid whatever characterization categories develop.

Most authors who explore problems at the intersection of law and science frame the issue in terms of how rapidly scientific information changes and how slowly the legal system responds. Others describe how the legal system distorts scientific information. These perspectives are important for understanding the relationship of law and science. Nevertheless, the problems go beyond misinterpretation and misuse of scientific information. This book argues that core problems at the intersection of law and science flow not from the changing nature of science but from the changing nature of law.

---

3 *See* Brian Greene, THE FABRIC OF THE COSMOS 96–98 (2004) (explaining that the uncertainty principle says that measuring one feature of the subatomic realm, such as a particle's position, velocity, energy, or angular momentum, compromises the ability to have knowledge of the other features because the measurement itself alters the features being observed); MARTIN GOLDSTEIN & INGE F. GOLDSTEIN, HOW WE KNOW: AN EXPLORATION OF THE SCIENTIFIC PROCESS 221–22 (1980) (discussing the Heisenberg uncertainty principle).

Law is by its nature evolutionary and adaptive. When we borrow structures from science, the adaptive process breaks down, and it does so for several reasons. The most obvious reason is that we do not understand the science we are importing or applying. As a result, we do not allow law to evolve in a very effective or nuanced fashion. Worse yet, we forget that scientific lines and categories are themselves no more than constructs. They are ways of developing groupings that create shared understandings within the scientific community. Such constructs can help scientists discuss and investigate a natural phenomenon. In a legal context, however, we easily lose sight of the artificiality and the assumptions that such constructs embody. The process of adaptation and evolution cannot unfold with great efficacy if it is supported by constructs whose weaknesses we fail to comprehend.

In our efforts to elevate law through incorporation of science, we succumb to the temptation to analogize too loosely to scientific concepts. The legal realists had very little understanding of Einstein's insights into physics, for example, but they were quick to borrow the notion of "relativity" for describing legal analysis, cloaking their legal reasoning in a reference to the scientific advancement of the time.[4]

---

4 Joel R. Cornwell, *From Hedonism to Human Rights: Felix Cohen's Alternative to Nihilism*, 68 TEMP. L. REV. 197, 208–09 (1995) (noting that "[t]he legal realists had grasped this significant feature of Einstein's theory of relativity. Just as there could be no motion apart from space and time, so there could be no law apart from emotions, instincts, and the entire range of economic, social, and political forces which compose a culture. Every legal decision was at bottom an ethical decision, not a neutral deduction from precedential mandates 'discovered' in the nature of things"); *cf.* BOSTON STUDIES IN THE PHILOSOPHY OF SCIENCE, THE NATURAL SCIENCES AND THE SOCIAL SCIENCES: SOME CRITICAL AND HISTORICAL PERSPECTIVES 61 (I. Bernard Cohen ed., 1994) [hereinafter BOSTON STUDIES] (explaining how the social scientist Carey, who sought to construct a science of society based on Newtonian celestial mechanics got the law of gravity wrong and describing the implications for those who emulate

In addition to breakdown in the process of evolution and adaptation, reaching for science so often fails because science simply cannot answer law's problems. Science can tell us the ways in which things are the same and the ways in which they differ, but it cannot tell us whether that sameness or difference should have any meaning from a legal perspective.

Consider the problem of determining the legitimacy of a tort injury, particularly one that involves pain. In a number of tort cases, injured parties assert that they are unable to work because of pain. In classic cases of illegitimate claims, the cases fall apart when the injured parties are captured on camera lifting heavy grocery bags, driving, and so forth. Modern research on brain patterns in response to pain offers the tantalizing possibility that courts could rely on scientific methods to determine whether an individual is experiencing pain.

The question, however, is not as simple as reading the results of a brain scan. Even if the pain is "real" in the sense that the individual experiences it, society might still not choose to respond. For example, individuals can be hypnotized into feeling pain, even if that pain was not caused by the injury. In that case, the pain experience would be demonstrable, yet it might not be an experience of pain that would give the injured person the right to tort compensation. In other words, even reliable pain measurement does not answer the question of where the pain comes from or whether it is compensable. Brain patterns can tell us whether the patterns

---

various sciences without sufficiently understanding the science they claim to be replicating); *id.* at 4 (noting that some economists whose ideas are still part of the foundations of modern economics, emulated a form of physics that is now outmoded, having been replaced by theories such as relativity and quantum mechanics).

are consistent with the experience of pain, but not whether that consistency is something the law should recognize.

Science rules may not work well for providing answers to law's questions, but they do provide something else. Relying on science gives us a delightfully convenient way to avoid the problems in front of us. In so many circumstances, we use science to create the Illusion of Reasonable Resolution where the solution is not reasoned nor is the issue resolved. Science allows us to ignore the fact that we have failed to resolve anything, or it allows us to mask the preferences embodied in the outcome. It relieves us of the psychic pressure of having to decide as well as the pressure of having to take responsibility for the decisions we have made or failed to make.[5]

Such an approach might have advantages. If one cannot solve an issue, why not ignore it or at least camouflage it? The problem, of course, is that the issues remain unresolved. They are doomed to reappear, sometimes in even more intractable form as we try to manage the additional confusions created by what we have imported. Thus, when we gain authority by obscurity, the process inevitably backfires leaving more chaos and confusion in the doctrines.

---

5 *See* Martha L. Fineman & Annie Opie, *The Uses of Social Science Data in Legal Policymaking: Custody Determinations at Divorce*, 1987 WISC. L. REV.107, 125 (arguing that social science data may be used as a substitute for a critical inquiry into the assumptions behind the policy choices); *see also* David M. Trubek, *Where the Action is: Critical Legal Studies and Empiricism*, 36 STAN. L. REV. 575, 618 (1984) (noting the CLS critique that social science methods hide an implicit and conservative political message behind a neutral and technocratic facade); *cf.* Jerome Frank, LAW & THE MODERN MIND 172 (1963) (noting that the suspense required to arrive at adequate judgment is painful, therefore the judge whose judgment is routine is avoiding the pain of suspended judgment).

Although the following chapters provide a number of examples in which law tries unsuccessfully to solve its problems through science, let me offer a brief summary of one at this point. It is an example of internalization, that is, importing scientific lines to resolve a legal dilemma. The dilemma concerns the law related to patenting genes. The full discussion of this example in Chapter II explains genetic inventions and describes the challenges inherent in defining the boundaries of those inventions. For introductory purposes, however, it is sufficient to note that the Federal Circuit sidestepped a number of difficult questions in this area of law more than a decade ago by choosing the following simple scientific line.[6] Genes are made up of nucleotide building blocks. In essence, the court said, "Give us the nucleotide sequence and we will give you the gene, no matter how simple the procedures are for moving from the current information to that sequence."[7]

With these decisions, the court adopted a clean, simple line based on a scientific marker to try to resolve a series of extraordinarily complex issues. There is a certain appeal to this approach. If one has to develop categories related to scientific inventions, why not choose scientific lines? This body of case law has been remarkably unsuccessful and has

---

6 *See in re* Deuel, 51 F.3d 1552 (Fed. Cir. 1995); *in re* Bell, 991 F.2d 781 (Fed. Cir. 1993).

7 *See* Deuel, 51 F.3d at 1558 (holding that the gene described in the patent was not an obvious invention because the prior art did not specifically list or suggest the nucleotide sequence); National Research Council of the National Academies of Science, A PATENT SYSTEM FOR THE 21ST CENTURY 92 (Stephen A. Merrill, Richard C. Levin & Mark B. Myers eds., 2005) [hereinafter NATIONAL ACADEMIES] (noting that the court in Bell and Deuel created a per se rule that the obviousness of obtaining a gene can *never* be relevant to patentability).

received unrelenting criticism.[8] In some areas, the approach affords too much protection for genetic claims, protecting claims that fail to meet international standards for biotech inventions[9] or to satisfy the level of invention required for other types of inventions.[10] In other areas, the approach has led to underprotection of genetic inventions, sending shock waves through the biotech industry. Across the board, the resulting case law has been confused and chaotic.

The question for the purposes of the example is, where did the Federal Circuit go wrong? Perhaps they simply picked the wrong line. Maybe if we were better scientists, we could get it right. The example, however, demonstrates a deeper problem. The legal issues in this area cannot be answered effectively with any simple line, scientific or not. Courts wading into this area must engage in a complex analysis of the nature of the problem addressed by a particular invention, the extent of the advancement created by the invention, and the significance of any differences between

---

8 *See, e.g.*, Dan L. Burk & Mark A. Lemley, *Is Patent Law Technology Specific?*, 17 BERKELEY TECH. L.J. 1155, 1179–80 (2002); Anita Varma & David Abraham, *DNA is Different: Legal Obviousness and the Balance Between Biotech Inventors and the Market*, 9 HARV. J.L. & TECH. 53 (1996); PHILIPPE G. DUCOR, PATENTING THE RECOMBINANT PRODUCTS OF BIOTECHNOLOGY (1998); Arti K. Rai, *Intellectual Property Rights in Biotechnology: Addressing New Technology*, 34 WAKE FOREST L. REV. 827 (1999); Arti K. Rai, *Addressing the Patent Gold Rush: The Role of Deference to PTO Patent Denials*, 2 WASH. U.J.L. & POL'Y 199 (2000); Univ. of Rochester v. G.D. Searle & Co., 375 F.3d 1303, 1314 (Fed. Cir. 2004) (Rader, J., dissenting to the denial of review en banc) (listing 31 academic articles criticizing the Lilly decision).

9 *See* NATIONAL ACADEMIES, *supra* note 7, at 93 (criticizing the American doctrine and noting that all other industrialized countries approach the nonobviousness of novel genes by focusing on the technical hurdles the inventor faces).

10 *See* Dan L. Burk & Mark A. Lemley, *Is Patent Law Technology Specific?*, 17 BERKELEY TECH. L.J. 1155, 1183–85 (2002) (arguing that the Federal Circuit's standards differ for biotechnology and software).

the advancement and later inventions. These are not bright line questions.

As bad as it is to throw in a rigid line where it does not belong, it is particularly problematic to throw in a scientific line. Legal actors tend to fixate on such lines, forgetting that the scientific line itself is an artificial construct that may or may not be appropriate as the legal issues evolve. Either we do not understand that scientific lines are constructs or we lose sight of the assumptions in those constructs, either one of which makes for ineffective analysis as case law unfolds.

Even the notion of a gene is an artificial construct. Cells contain strands of DNA. Genes are simply locations on that strand. In other words, the idea of a gene is a way of conceptualizing a continuous string as if it were broken up into pieces. It is a very useful way for scientists to talk about and explore genetic phenomena. Nevertheless, the legal system is assigning rights to those pieces. If we lose sight of the assumptions and the artificiality involved, we lose the ability to ask coherently whether the scientific line fits the legal issues properly as those issues unfold in the cases.

One can frame the problem in terms of forgetting, that is, we forget that science lines have their own assumptions and artificiality. Alternatively, one could frame the problem in terms of abdicating. Having reached for a scientific solution, one that we do not fully understand, we stop taking responsibility for analyzing it, challenging it, and adapting it in later cases. Whether the problem is forgetting or abdicating, the result is truncated legal analysis and doctrinal areas that become increasingly confused. The legal process simply does not work effectively.

Gene patents offer an example of internalization of science. This book looks at other examples of internalization as well as examples in which law tries to externalize its dilemmas.

In both settings, we allow ourselves to believe that law's problems will dissolve if we turn to science.

This is not to suggest that the law should ignore what science has to offer. Science has been and can be enormously helpful to the legal system. The question is how to effectively manage the role that science can play. This book describes a variety of ways to manage the interaction of law and science more effectively, but let me summarize one of the current examples here. It is an antitrust example that arises out of the legislation that regulates the entry of generic drugs into the market. The legislation encourages companies to reduce the price of medications by creating generic drugs and challenging bad patents. The notion, in highly simplified form, is that the first company that files for approval of a generic drug and challenges either the validity of the patent on that drug or the application of the patent to its generic version receives a six-month exclusivity period in which to sell the generic drug.[11] No other company can sell a generic version of the drug until six months after the initial challenger finally gets to market. The scheme is intended to give generic companies an incentive to enter the fray and battle the many ways in which patent holders maneuver to keep generics off the market.

Patent holders, however, are by nature quite creative. Some have entered into settlements with the generic challenger in which the patent holder pays the generic and the generic agrees to stay out of the market for a period of years. The settlement is a great deal for the generic. The generic

11 For a more complete description of the legislative scheme, *see* text accompanying notes 397–428; *see also* Matthew Avery, Note, *Continuing Abuse of the Hatch-Waxman Act by Pharmaceutical Patent Holders and the Failure of the 2003 Amendments*, 60 HASTINGS L.J. (forthcoming 2008) (providing a tremendously thorough account of the Hatch-Waxman legislation and its effects).

gets paid and does not have to pursue the lawsuit. Most important, when the generic finally enters the market, it will still receive the full six-month exclusivity period because the six-month clock does not start ticking until the first challenger actually gets to market. If the patent is weak or invalid, the settlement also is good for the patent holder. The patent holder is able to hold onto its monopoly by sharing a portion of its monopoly returns with the challenger. It is a neat deal, and one that economics would suggest could be problematic for the consumer.

How should a court respond to such settlements? On the one hand, there is tremendous potential for anticompetitive collusion. On the other hand, settlements play an important role in the litigation process, embodying judgments about the costs and risks of further litigation even when a case is quite strong. Law and economics scholars have suggested a variety of approaches, including that courts should allow such settlements when the settlement would generate at least as much consumer surplus as consumers would have enjoyed had the settlement not been reached and the dispute had been resolved through litigation instead. The proposal provides an elegant solution to a complex problem, using economics to give courts a rule to live by. Living by that rule, however, requires the type of complicated economic calculation that courts simply are not very good at engaging in with any degree of accuracy or precision. If courts are unable to measure with any degree of accuracy, why is the legal system adopting this type of rule?

The fact that courts cannot measure with confidence, however, does not mean that we abandon the insights of economics in crafting a solution. A variety of solutions are possible that would realign the incentives of the parties to make it less likely they would choose to collude. In particular, courts could adopt rules that permit such settlements only if the patent holder is likely to succeed on the merits of the case. Likelihood of success on the merits is a calculation that courts are much better suited to engaging in than comparing consumer surplus amounts in two hypothetical settings. In short, we can use the insights of economics to resolve the legal dilemma not by crafting measurements for the court to apply or by deferring to economists to do the measuring but in a way that allows courts to engage in the type of analysis that courts are good at.

This is not to suggest that all measurement should be excised from legal tests or that all problems can be solved by aligning the incentives of the parties with society's incentives. The point is that the more we can stick to rules reflecting the types of tasks law is designed to accomplish, the better results we can expect.

As a general framework, this book separates law's attempts to reach for science into two forms. In one form, legal actors try to adopt the mantle of science themselves. When faced with difficult legal dilemmas, courts may try to solve the problem by taking a scientific line or category and inserting it into the legal doctrine. After all, if law has to develop lines and create categories somehow, why not borrow from scientific fields where there is at least a studied, rational basis for the groupings? In other examples, we ask science to tell us something to measure and place that measurement into the doctrine. In the most extreme version, we try to make law itself into a science, reconceptualizing law to conform to our notion of what would make law more scientific. One can think of this set of approaches as internalization of science into law. In the second form of reaching for science, we try to export law's problems to science, endowing experts with the power to decide legal questions. One can think of this approach as externalization. Thus, at times we try to import science into law; at other times, we try to export the problems of law to science.

Both strategies frequently fail, but they are exquisitely revealing. They reflect a persistent image of law as weak and ineffective, a pale shadow in its own domain of what the sciences can project in theirs. It is this distorted imagery that leads courts repeatedly into the same types of traps. The challenge for modern legal scholars is to understand how our image of law and science becomes distorted and how we can adjust that vision to find a more effective intersection for the two domains.

Chapter II explores examples of internalization in modern law. The chapter begins by examining internalization of scientific markers in abortion cases and law's reluctance to abandon those markers as they prove inadequate for resolving the issues. The chapter then examines the use of scientific lines in Internet searching cases and the inevitable failure of the technical distinctions chosen. Finally, it explores the example described above concerning gene patent cases.

Chapter III explores examples of externalization, in which modern law tries to outsource its dilemmas to experts. It begins by examining a 2006 Supreme Court decision concerning property rights and environmental law. Justice Kennedy's concurring opinion in that case provides a classic example of trying to resolve a legal problem by calling for experts to parse through scientific distinctions, when those distinctions were beside the point in the case. The chapter then examines debates in modern antitrust law between Chicago School and post-Chicago scholars, which reflect concerns over whether courts have the ability to apply sophisticated economic analysis. The battle lines in these debates do not necessarily fall where one would expect.

Having looked at examples of internalization and externalization in modern law, the book then turns to the historic record. Chapter IV traces the instinct to reach for science in American legal doctrine back through the 1800s. It examines both the more formal legal theory movements as well as individual doctrinal moments in which American law reaches for science in an attempt to solve its problems and is disappointed when the solution fails to live up to its promise. The chapter begins by describing various attempts to reconceptualize law as a science in the pre-Civil War period and the failure of those attempts in the wake of the Civil War. The chapter then describes reinvigoration of the "law as science" idea in the 1870s as Christopher Langdell popularizes the notion, leaving an enduring mark on American legal education. Next, variations on the concept of law as a science in legal theory movements of the 1900s are explored. This part discusses the rise of the administrative state in the early twentieth century, as well as the theories of the progressives, the legal realists, the legal process school, law and economics, and critical legal studies.

The chapter then turns to individual doctrinal moments in which American law has reached for science to solve intractable problems and is subsequently disappointed. The examples explored include criminal law doctrines related to finding a defendant not guilty by reason of insanity, civil law doctrines related to the best interests of the child in custody cases, the Supreme Court's desegregation decision in *Brown v. Board of Education*, the Learned Hand test for negligence liability in tort law, and rate setting in public utility regulation.

Chapter V of the book addresses the nature of law. It explores the way in which societal change and human nature drive law toward the open spaces created by existing doctrinal structures. The chapter then considers and rejects the notion that law related to technology might require a different role for science. It compares the process of patent interpretation to constitutional interpretation, noting that in both settings, the law is trying to interpret the extent of rights granted with a document in the context of rapidly changing meaning and knowledge. Science, whether biochemistry or linguistics, can offer only limited assistance in such an enterprise. The chapter then describes the process of law as an expression of Bounded Adaptation in which those adaptations are evaluated within the prevailing norms of the relevant sphere of acceptance. The chapter concludes by exploring how internalization and externalization of science are ill suited to law's process of adaptation.

Chapter VI of the book explores the nature of science as a prelude to understanding how law's distorted image of science exacerbates problems at the intersection of the two realms. The chapter describes the development of science as a separate intellectual discipline, focusing on three periods of history that are critical to the development of the law/science relationship: ancient Greece, the Scientific Revolution in Europe, and twentieth century reevaluations of the definition of science.

Chapter VII explains that the revolution in modern views of science has gone largely unnoticed in law. It discusses how our failure to understand the limitations of science creates distortions in the legal system as we forge ahead trying to let science solve our problems. In this context, the chapter looks at past misuse of scientific or pseudo-scientific evidence as well as the potential for future misuse of evidence related to modern technologies such as fMRI.

The chapter also describes the value of including social science in the category of the sciences for which we reach in law. This grouping is important for understanding the instinct within law to look for the "authoritative other," something external to law that we interpret as having superior reliability. Although American law has reached for many forms of authoritative other across the centuries, including history, philosophy, and theology, the dangers are particularly great when the authoritative other is grounded in concepts that legal actors do not thoroughly comprehend. Social science, as well as hard science, fits within that category, and our internalization and externalization attempts follow familiar patterns in both.

Finally, Chapter VIII suggests how to make law and science work together more effectively within the domain of law. This section argues that the key is not to rest legal rules on scientific lines or measurements but to use the insights of science for aligning incentives and testing assumptions underlying the legal rules we choose. In addition, where the legal system interacts with science, we must move toward speaking in a common language, one that will be susceptible to the process of interpretation and adaptation that is essential to law. Most important, the chapter argues that we are unlikely to avoid the cycles of exaltation and disappointment unless we are willing to embrace the imperfections of law. It is our misguided yearning for completeness and perfection in law that drives us to look for rescue in the form of science.

CHAPTER II

Internalization of Science in Modern Law

[Our aim] is to encourage the application of scientific methods to the study of the legal system. As biology is to living organisms, astronomy to the stars, or economics to the price system, so should legal studies be to the legal system.

Richard Posner[12]

Law's attempts to reach for science can be separated into two essential forms. In one form, legal actors try to adopt the mantle of science. We craft legal rules based on scientific lines of demarcation or cloak ourselves in scientific jargon for shelter and comfort. In the most extreme expression of adopting the mantle of science, we try to reconceptualize law itself to transform it into a science or at least to make it more scientific. One can think of these examples as internalizing science into law.[13]

---

12 Richard Posner, *Afterword*, 1 J. LEGAL STUD. 437 (1972).

13 For other perspectives on the interrelation of law and science, *see* Roscoe Pound, *Law and the Science of Law in Recent Theories*, 43 YALE. L. REV. 525 (1934); DAVID FAIGMAN, LEGAL ALCHEMY: THE USE AND ABUSE OF SCIENCE IN THE LAW (1999); Ronald Dworkin, *Social Sciences and Constitutional Right—the Consequences of Uncertainty*, J. L. & ED., Vol. 6, No. 1, at 3 (1977); Steven Goldberg, *The Reluctant Embrace: Law and Science in America*, 75 GEO. L.J. 1341 (1987); Dean Hashimoto, *Science as Mythology in Constitutional Law*, 76 OR. L. REV. 111 (1997); Oliver Wendell Holmes, *Law in Science and Science in*

In another form of reaching for science, law simply defers to scientists, endowing scientists and other experts with the power to decide legal questions that we despair of answering

---

Law, 12 HARV. L. REV. 443 (1899); Richard Lempert, *"Between Cup and Lip": Social Science Influences on Law and Policy*, LAW & POLICY, Vol. 10, No. 2 & 3 at 167 (1988); Karl N. Llewellyn, *The Theory of Legal "Science,"* 20 N.C. L. REV. 1 (1942); Howard T. Markey, *Jurisprudence or "Juriscience"?*, 25 WM. & MARY L. REV. 525 (1984); J. Alexander Tanford, *The Limits of a Scientific Jurisprudence: The Supreme Court and Psychology*, 66 IND. L.J. 137 (1991); Charles R. Tremper, *Sanguinity and Disillusionment Where Law Meet Social Science*, LAW & HUMAN BEHAVIOR, Vol. 11, No. 4, at 267 (1987); John Veilleux, Note, *The Scientific Model in Law*, 75 GEO. L.J. 1967 (1987). For perspectives on American Legal Theories in general, *see* NEIL DUXBURY, PATTERNS OF AMERICAN JURISPRUDENCE (1995); MARK KELMAN, A GUIDE TO CRITICAL LEGAL STUDIES (1987); GARY MINDA, POSTMODERN LEGAL MOVEMENTS: LAW AND JURISPRUDENCE AT CENTURY'S END (1995); JOHN HENRY SCHLEGEL, AMERICAN LEGAL REALISM AND EMPIRICAL SOCIAL SCIENCE (1995); ANTHONY J. SEBOK, LEGAL POSITIVISM IN AMERICAN JURISPRUDENCE (1998); Guido Calabresi, *An Introduction to Legal Thought: Four Approaches to Law and to the Allocation of Body Parts*, 55 STAN. L. REV. 2113 (2003); Ronald Dworkin, *The Model of Rules*, 35 U. CHI. L. REV. 14 (1967); Thomas C. Grey, *Langdell's Orthodoxy*, 45 U. PITT. L. REV. 1 (1983) [hereinafter Grey, *Langdell's Orthodoxy*]; Herbert Hovenkamp, *Positivism in Law & Economics*, 78 CAL. L. REV. 815 (1990) [hereinafter Hovenkamp, *Positivism*]; Avery Wiener Katz, *Positivism and the Separation of Law and Economics*, 94 MICH. L. REV. 2229 (1996); Arthur Allen Leff, *Law and*, 87 YALE L.J. 989 (1978); Martha C. Nussbaum, *The Use and Abuse of Philosophy in Legal Education*, 45 STAN. L. REV. 1627 (1993); Richard Posner, *Legal Scholarship Today*, 45 STAN. L. REV. 1647 (1993); Edward L. Rubin, *Law and the Methodology of Law*, 1997 WIS. L. REV. 521 (1997); Austin Sarat & Jonathan Simon, *Beyond Legal Realism?: Cultural Analysis, Cultural Studies, and the Situation of Legal Scholarship*, 13 YALE J.L. & HUMAN. 3 (2001); Howard Schweber, "*Langdell, We Hardly Knew Ye,*" 17 LAW & HIST. REV. 145 (1999); *see also* Edgar S. Cahn, *An Anthropologist Examines the Lawyer Tribe*, 17 YALE J.L. & HUMAN. 291 (2005); Daniel R. Ernst, *The Lost Law Professor*, 21 LAW & SOC. INQUIRY 967 (1996). Brian Bix, *Positively Positivism*, 85 VA. L. REV. 889 (1999); Thomas C. Grey, *Modern American Legal Thought*, 106 YALE L.J. 493 (1996); Christopher L. Sagers, Book Note, 95 MICH. L. REV. 1927 (1997) [hereinafter Grey, *Modern American Legal Thought*] (reviewing GARY MINDA, POSTMODERN LEGAL MOVEMENTS: LAW AND JURISPRUDENCE AT CENTURY'S END (1995).

ourselves. Thus, in some circumstances, we try to internalize science into law, and in other circumstances, we try to externalize the problems of law. This chapter describes the internalization of science in modern law.

A. ABORTION

A classic example of internalization of science can be found in abortion cases, where the courts tried to use science markers to solve an intractable legal dilemma. Faced with the most contentious areas of modern American law, courts reached for a simple scientific line to try to resolve tensions among the interests of the mother, the interests of the fetus, the interests of physicians, and society's interests related to all of these. Specifically, the federal courts in *Roe v. Wade* and its progeny settled into dividing lines based on conceptualizing pregnancy in three trimesters.[14] In the first trimester, the state

14 *See* Planned Parenthood v. Casey, 505 U.S. 833, 872 (1992) (discussing and rejecting the "rigid" trimester approach of *Roe* and its progeny); *see also* Roe v. Wade, 410 U.S. 113 (1973). *Roe* actually focused more on viability than the line between the second and third trimester, but subsequent cases, scholarship, and legislation focused on the third trimester line as well as *Roe's* line between the first and second trimester. *See* Planned Parenthood v. Casey, 505 U.S. 833, 873 (arguing that the trimester line was not part of the essential holding of Roe); Roe v. Wade, 410 U.S. at 163–64 (focusing on the first/second trimester line and the viability line); *see also* Doe v. Bolton, 410 U.S. 179, 195 (1973) (invalidating a Georgia law that required abortions to be performed in hospitals on the grounds that the law failed to exclude abortions performed during the first trimester of pregnancy); Connecticut v. Menillo, 423 U.S. 9, 11 (1975) (although upholding Connecticut's criminal abortion statutes against nonphysicians, the court reiterated that *Roe* preserves a woman's right to terminate her pregnancy during the first trimester because a State's interest in maternal health or in the fetus' potential life is insufficient at that stage to regulate the pregnancy); Simopoulos v. Virginia, 462 U.S. 506, 517 (1983) (upholding a Virginia law which required second trimester abortions to be performed in licensed clinics since the regulation

could not intervene.[15] In the second trimester, the state could intervene on the theory that the risk of harm to the mother from abortion matched or exceeded the risk of harm to the mother from childbirth.[16] Finally, in the third trimester, the state could intervene in the interests of protecting the fetus.[17] Rather than providing an authoritative and acceptable resolution, the scientific line was assailed from both the right and the left from its inception. It was abandoned decades later by a Supreme Court decision acknowledging that both the mother and the state have interests throughout the gestational period.[18]

The scientific line was doomed from the start, given that it ignored the fundamental philosophical issues. No scientific line could ever resolve the underlying questions of when life begins, how we should treat even potential life, and what forum is the correct one in which to address the issues. These excruciatingly difficult legal issues were bound to persist, despite any efforts to find an "objective" scientific line.

Suppose that science advanced to the point at which life could be developed and sustained outside the womb at the moment of conception. It would be difficult to imagine that pro-choice advocates would simply abandon their position

---

did not impinge on the woman's right to terminate her pregnancy during the first trimester).

15 *See* Planned Parenthood v. Casey, 505 U.S. at 872; Roe v. Wade, 410 U.S. at 163.

16 *See id.*

17 *See* Planned Parenthood v. Casey, 505 U.S. at 872.

18 *See id.* at 872–73. The mother's interest was already recognized as existing throughout the gestational period but deemed outweighed in the third trimester by the state's compelling interest in protecting the fetus, except where the life of the mother is at stake. The State's interest was not recognized as existing throughout the gestational period until the trimester line was abandoned.

and support a complete ban on abortion. The questions are far more complex than any scientific line could ever hope to resolve.

The trimester line was not only unsatisfactory from a philosophical standpoint, it was also inadequate from a scientific standpoint. Nevertheless, the trimester line remained as a point of fixation even as the safety point for the mother to have an abortion moved later than the first trimester and the viability point for the fetus moved earlier than the third trimester.[19] Having grabbed onto a scientific marker, the law continued to cling to it, even as it failed to comport with medical science. The simple scientific line was a failure, but it took decades to abandon it.

B. COPYRIGHT

Other examples of internalization can be found in modern copyright cases, which vividly demonstrate law's penchant for technological line drawing. Consider a 2006 district court opinion granting an injunction against the search engine company Google for displaying thumbnail images as part of its search results.[20] When someone enters a search on Google, the results may include a tiny image from the Web sites that Google offers as search results. The legal question

---

19 *See, e.g.*, Hashimoto, *supra* note 13, at 144–45 (complaining that the Supreme Court in *City of Akron v. Akron Center for Reproductive Health* confronted substantial data which indicated that abortions were safer than normal childbirth at up to sixteen weeks, well beyond the end of the first trimester); *see also* City of Akron v. Akron Ctr. for Reproductive Health, 462 U.S. 416 (1983);City of Akron v. Akron Ctr. for Reproductive Health, 462 U.S. 416, 458 n.5 (1983) (noting that recent studies had documented increasingly early viability).

20 *See* Perfect 10 v. Google, Inc. 416 F. Supp. 2d 838 (C.D. Cal. 2006), *rev'd sub nom* Perfect 10 v. Amazon, Inc., 487 F.3d 701 (9th Cir. 2007).

concerns whether Google has violated copyright law by making and displaying an unauthorized copy of something from the Web site. The Google case is one of a number of cases concerning "linking," that is, when a Web site or a search engine displays information from another web site.[21]

The district court ruled that the legality of Google's actions turned on whether the images Google displayed were ever technically on Google's servers rather than only residing on the Web site to which Google provides a link.[22] This distinction echoes a line the Ninth Circuit hinted at when it withdrew an earlier opinion concerning linking.[23]

Once again, what looks like a simple, objective, scientific line completely misses the point. A technical distinction of this kind cannot possibly help the law come to terms with the question of how to respect copyright holders' rights while still adapting to the increased interconnectivity of Web sites and the role of search engines in our daily lives. These issues will continue to haunt the legal system as further cases emerge, and the *Google* decision will be of little help. Shelter cannot be found in grasping for technological dividing lines, although examples abound in copyright law.[24]

---

21 *See Perfect 10*, 416 F. Supp. 2d at 838–843; *see also* Kelly v. Arriba Soft Corp., 336 F.3d 811, 816 (9th Cir. 2003); Playboy Enters., Inc. v. Webbworld, Inc., 991 F. Supp. 543 (N.D. Tex. 1997); Playboy Enters., Inc. v. Russ Hardenburgh, Inc., 982 F. Supp. 503 (N.D. Ohio 1997); Online Policy Group v. Diebold, Inc., 337 F. Supp. 2d 1195, 1202 n.12 (N.D. Cal. 2004).

22 *See id.* at 10–11, 13.

23 *See id.* at 10–11 (describing Kelly v. Arriba); *see also* Kelly v. Arriba Soft Corp., 336 F.3d 811, 816 (9th Cir. 2003), *amending* 280 F.3d 93 (9th Cir. 2002).

24 Another example of technological line drawing in copyright cases can be found in Metro-Goldwyn-Mayer Studios, Inc. v. Grokster Ltd., 380 F.3d 1154, 1165–66 (9th Cir. 2004), *reversed and remanded*, 125 S. Ct 2764 (2005) (ruling that the legality of a peer-to-peer file sharing service, turned on whether the transferred files resided on the defendant's servers).

The problem of using technological lines to resolve difficult legal issues also appears in cases related to format-shifting in music.[25] A persistent problem for the courts in modern copyright cases is the fundamental difference between the way consumers view the products they purchase and the way the entertainment industry views those products. When consumers buy a CD, for example, they expect to be able to listen to it on their stereo at home, on their iPod as they move around, or on their MP3 player in the car.[26]

---

25 *See* Joint Reply Comments of Association of American Publishers et al. at 31, Exemption to Prohibition on Circumvention of Copyright Protection Systems for Access Control Technologies, No. RM 2005–11 (filed Feb. 2, 2006), *available at* http://www.copyright.gov/1201/2006/reply/11metalitz_AAP.pdf (on file with author) (arguing that "The Register was right in 2003 to be 'skeptical' of the merits of any fair use analysis that asserts that space-shifting or format-shifting is a noninfringing use"); *see also* RIAA.com, *Piracy: Online and On the Streets—The Law*, http://www.riaa.com/physicalpiracy.php?content_selector=piracy_online_the_law (last visited June 11, 2008) (on file with author). The RIAA does not explicitly acknowledge that encoding a legally purchased audio CD into MP3 files is fair use. *See id.* (stating that "mak[ing] an MP3 copy of a song because the CD you bought *expressly* permits you to do so" is legal, implying that express permission is required (emphasis added)).

26 Even outside the file-sharing context, the Recording Industry Association of America (RIAA) has made claims that changing the format of legally purchased music, even for use by the original purchaser, is infringement. At the well-publicized trial of Jammie Thomas, "Sony BMG's chief of litigation, Jennifer Pariser, testified that 'when an individual makes a copy of a song for himself, I suppose we can say he stole a song.'" Marc Fisher, *Download Uproar: Record Industry Goes After Personal Use*, WASHINGTON POST, Dec. 1, 2007, http://www.washingtonpost.com/wp-dyn/content/article/2007/12/28/AR2007122800693.html (last visited June 4, 2008). *See also* RIAA.com, *Piracy, supra* note 26 (stating that beyond copying music onto special Audio CD-Rs, which include a royalty as part of the purchase price, "there's no legal "right" to copy the copyrighted music on a CD onto a CD-R. However, burning a copy of CD onto a CD-R, or transferring a copy onto your computer hard drive or your portable music player, won't *usually* raise concerns" (emphasis added).

To consumers, it is a product they have purchased, and they ought to be able to enjoy it anytime, anywhere, and through any type of technology.

Some consumers would go even further, expecting that they should be able to share a song or a game they like with a friend by beaming it to them across hand-held devices or over the Internet. The recording industry, however, has gone to great lengths in recent years to disabuse consumers of the notion that sharing is legitimate. In fact, the entertainment industry views the sale of a CD in entirely different terms from consumers. To the entertainment industry, a CD embodies a license to listen to the song in limited circumstances, through particular technology, and perhaps even with limitations in the number of times or the length of time one can enjoy the right to listen to the song. As a result, the entertainment industry views shifting your song from one technology to another, such as transferring music from a CD that you own to your iPod, as infringement, although this news will come as a shock to most consumers. Similarly, the entertainment industry argues that making backup copies of anything is infringement. From their perspective, one could argue that if your CD breaks or gets scratched, it reflects a natural and built-in limitation on the length of time that one has been granted the right to hear the song. Consumers, therefore, should not be allowed to make backup copies to extend the natural obsolescence. Along the same lines, the entertainment industry certainly views sharing a copy with a friend as infringement. These visions of what one can reasonably expect when buying a copy of a creative work stand in sharp contrast to the views of most consumers. It is this underlying conflict that drives numerous modern copyright cases.

Courts addressing these issues, however, tend to cling to narrow technological dividing lines. Consider, for example, the MP3.com case that was decided in 2000. The case concerned the legality of a service that allowed people who legitimately own a copy of a CD to access that music anywhere they had an Internet connection.[27] The abstract concept was that music owners could essentially store their legitimately purchased CDs in a virtual music locker, which could then be accessed through the MP3.com Internet service.

The district court found that the service constituted copyright infringement. The decision rested on the fact that the consumer's own CD was not actually transmitted across the Internet. Rather, once MP3.com verified that the consumer owned a copy of the CD, the service transmitted files from its own library, which was then ruled a commercial transfer without a license.[28] By taking this approach, the court allowed the technical question of how files moved and where they were stored to trump any consideration of the deeper issues at work concerning whether it is reasonable for consumers to shift their music to different forums and different locations for personal use. We cannot solve the fundamental conflicts between consumers and the entertainment industry, however, by calibrating ever finer technological lines. Resolution does not lurk in lines of computer code.

C. GENE PATENTS

In no area of law is there a greater temptation to use science then in patent law. This is not surprising given that the subject matter of patent law is science itself. If nowhere else,

27 *See* UMG Recordings, Inc. v. MP3.com, Inc., 92 F. Supp. 2d 349, 351 (S.D.N.Y. 2000). MP3 technology allows for the compression of compact disc (CD) audio into computer files, which do not require the physical CD to play. *See id.*

28 *See id.*

surely it must be appropriate to incorporate science in an area of law that involves defining a scientific invention?

The task we engage in when we define an invention by interpreting a patent, however, is the same as the task we engage in throughout law as we interpret precedent. The essence of both involves interpreting the meaning of language and the boundaries of that language in ever-changing circumstances.[29] Rather than acknowledging the commonality, however, modern patent law consistently hides behind scientific lines of demarcation and science jargon in an effort to resolve difficult legal questions. Once again, the failure to grasp the nettles of our legal quandaries creates chaos in the doctrines.[30]

Consider the Federal Circuit's struggles with the question of how to properly identify the boundaries of a genetic invention. One might imagine that genes are physically separate items in a human cell, like pennies or nickels that one could pick up individually and identify the boundaries in both a physical and conceptual manner. Such is not the case at all. Human cells contain strands of DNA.[31] Genes are simply segments of those DNA strands. We designate segments of the strand as a "gene" based on what that segment does, and we assign legal rights to what is essentially a segment of a string.

If patent law grants rights in new inventions, how can a scientist claim rights to a gene in the first place? The scientist certainly did not invent the gene. The gene already exists in the human body. Patent law, however, allows inventors to claim rights in something that occurs in nature when the

29 *See infra* Chapter V, Part B (comparing patent interpretation with Constitutional interpretation).

30 *See infra* note 112 (referencing H.L.A. Hart).

31 *See* Karl Drlica, Understanding DNA and Gene Cloning 3 (3d ed. 1997).

substance has been isolated and purified from its natural state in a way that allows a new and practical use.[32] Thus, when a scientist succeeds in identifying, isolating, and purifying a gene, the scientist can claim rights in that gene outside the state of nature, as long as the scientist can satisfy the other requirements of patentability.[33]

One of those other requirements is proof that the invention is nonobvious. In other words, an inventor must show that creation of the invention would not have been a perfectly obvious step for those skilled in the relevant art. In the case of genes, how do we determine whether a scientist claiming rights in a particular gene has engaged in enough creative and inventive activity to claim an invention? Does it matter if the techniques for isolating genes are already known? Does it matter if techniques for isolating genes *and* substantial information about the gene or its products are already known?[34] How much must an inventor contribute?

32 *See* Parke-Davis & Co. v. H.K. Mulford Co., 189 F. 95, 103 (S.D.N.Y. 1911), *aff'd*, 196 F. 496 (2d Cir. 1912). *See also* Merck & Co. v. Olin Mathieson Chem. Corp., 253 F.2d 156, 162 (4th Cir. 1958); Robin C. Feldman, *Rethinking Rights in Biospace*, 79 SO. CAL. L. REV. 1, 5–8 (describing the evolution of patent law that leads to patenting of genetic inventions).

33 *See* Amgen Inc. v. Hoechst Marion Roussel, Inc., 314 F.3d 1313, 1329 (Fed. Cir. 2003) (holding in a protein case that the scientist who isolated and identified the protein EPO had rights to EPO produced from any source and by any particular method other than the way nature intended); *see also* JANICE M. MUELLER, AN INTRODUCTION TO PATENT LAW (2003) (describing the 5 elements of patentability: proper subject matter, novelty, utility, nonobviousness, and adequate disclosure).

34 *See in re* Bell, 991 F.2d 781 (Fed. Cir. 1993); *see also in re* O'Farrell, 853 F.2d 894 (Fed. Cir. 1988) (noting that the general technology for identifying and isolating genes is already available).

The Federal Circuit sidestepped these difficult issues more than a decade ago by choosing a simple scientific line.[35] Genes are made up of nucleotide building blocks. In essence, the court said, "Give us the nucleotide sequence and we will give you the gene, no matter how simple the procedures are for moving from the current information to that sequence."[36] The Federal Circuit tried to impose a simple, scientific line to settle the conflicts.

The Federal Circuit took the same approach to other difficult issues regarding the patenting of genetic inventions. For example, assuming biotech inventors clear the nonobviousness hurdle, how can they sufficiently demonstrate that they actually have in hand what they claim to have invented? In addition, how should patent law define the limits of what the inventor has? Again, the Federal Circuit responded with the cry of "nucleotide sequence." Inventors would receive a patent only when they described the nucleotide sequence of the relevant gene (or the amino acid sequence of the relevant protein), and they would control anything with precisely that nucleotide sequence.[37]

With these decisions, the court adopted a clean, simple line based on a scientific marker to try to resolve a series of extraordinarily complex issues. This body of case law has

---

35 *See in re* Deuel, 51 F.3d 1552 (Fed. Cir. 1995); *in re* Bell, 991 F.2d 781 (Fed. Cir. 1993).

36 *See Deuel*, 51 F.3d at 1558 (holding that the gene described in the patent was not an obvious invention because the prior art did not specifically list or suggest the nucleotide sequence); *National Academies*, *supra* note 7, at 92 (noting that the court in *Bell* and *Deuel* created a per se rule that the obviousness of obtaining a gene can *never* be relevant to patentability).

37 *See Regents of the University of California v. Eli Lilly & Co.*, 119 F.3d 1559 (Fed. Cir. 1997); Enzo Biochem, Inc. v. Gen-Probe Inc., 285 F.3d, 1013 (Fed. Cir. 2002), *revised by See* Enzo Biochem, Inc. v. Gen-Probe Inc., 296 F.3d 1316, 1330 (Fed. Cir. 2002).

been remarkably unsuccessful and has received unrelenting criticism.[38] For example, in the area of nonobviousness, short circuiting the inquiry has distorted the results of cases, protecting genetic claims that fail to meet international standards for biotech inventions[39] or to satisfy the level of invention required for other types of inventions.[40]

---

38 *See, e.g.*, Anita Varma & David Abraham, *DNA is Different: Legal Obviousness and the Balance Between Biotech Inventors and the Market*, 9 HARV. J.L. & TECH. 53, 78 (1996) (noting that the *in re Deuel* decision "the reasoning in Deuel leaves a biotechnologist of ordinary skill in the art in an awkward position" and that "[a]fter Bell and Deuel, the protection balance has tilted too heavily against the first inventor to file a patent application, and also too far away from the market that has already had access to the publicly available information"); Arti K. Rai, *Intellectual Property Rights in Biotechnology: Addressing New Technology*, 34 WAKE FOREST L. REV. 827 (1999); Arti K. Rai, *Addressing the Patent Gold Rush: The Role of Deference to PTO Patent Denials*, 2 WASH. U.J.L. & POL'Y 199, 207 & n.20 (2000) (noting that *in re Bell* and *in re Deuel* failed to show deference to PTO denials of patentability); Stephen J. Burdick, *Moba v. Diamond Automation, Inc.: Questioning the Separate Written Description Requirement*, 19 Berkeley Tech. L.J. 133, 138 (2004) (noting that "Eli Lilly's free-standing disclosure requirement received an avalanche of criticisms. Thereafter, the Federal Circuit tried to limit the expansive application of the written description requirement"); Dan L. Burk & Mark A. Lemley, *Is Patent Law Technology Specific?*, 17 BERKELEY TECH. L.J. 1155, 1179–80 (2002) (stating that the *Bell* court "arguably just got the science wrong; by the time of the research at issue in Bell, such methods for searching a large universe of molecules were perhaps painstaking and time consuming, but had an established likelihood of success"); *see also* Univ. of Rochester v. G.D. Searle & Co., 375 F.3d 1303, 1314 (Fed. Cir. 2004) (Rader, J., dissenting to the denial of review en banc) (listing 31 academic articles criticizing the *Lilly* decision).

39 *See National Academies, supra* note 7, at 93 (criticizing the American doctrine and noting that all other industrialized countries approach the nonobviousness of novel genes by focusing on the technical hurdles faced by the inventor.).

40 *See* Dan L. Burk & Mark A. Lemley, *Is Patent Law Technology Specific?*, 17 Berkeley Tech. L.J. 1155, 1183–85 (2002) (arguing that the Federal Circuit's standards differ for biotechnology and software).

While the nucleotide sequence requirement asks for too little in some areas, it asks for too much in others. For example, as described above, the Federal Circuit declared that the question of whether an inventor actually has the claimed invention in hand turns on whether the inventor listed the nucleotide sequence in the patent application. This development sent chills through the biotech industry as inventors, who had routinely deposited their inventions in public data banks as proof of creation, watched the Federal Circuit invalidate their patents.[41] The *Enzo* case,[42] which implemented this principle, was withdrawn and reissued within a few months in response to a firestorm of criticism. *Enzo II*[43] reinstated the patent and tried to suggest a narrow area of

---

41 In addition, patent law allows inventors to claim a group of items based on information gained from identifying a limited number of members of the group. Requiring that inventors list nucleotide sequences, however, could suggest that inventors must on identify and list the sequence for every member of a group in order to claim the group. This creates tremendous tension between different doctrinal areas. For a general description of conflicts within this area of law, *see* Feldman, *Rethinking Rights, supra* note 32.

42 *See* Enzo Biochem, Inc. v. Gen-Probe Inc., 285 F.3d, 1013 (Fed. Cir. 2002) [hereinafter *Enzo I*], *revised by* Enzo Biochem, Inc. v. Gen-Probe Inc., 323 F.3d 956 (Fed. Cir. 2002) [hereinafter *Enzo II*].

43 *See Enzo II, supra* note 42, at 964 (suggesting that a written description of structural details of sequencing might not be necessary where sufficient correlation of structure and function exists); brief of Government as amicus curiae at 4–5 requesting en banc consideration in Enzo Biochem, Inc. v. Gen-Probe Inc., 323 F.3d 956 (Fed. Cir. 2002), *quoted in* Univ. of Rochester v. G.D. Searle & Co., 375 F.3d 1303, 1309 (Fed. Cir. 2004) (Rader, J., dissenting from denial of en banc) (noting that the Federal Circuit's decisions have not taken a clear and uniform position regarding the purpose and meaning of the requirements in the written description area); Univ. of Rochester v. G.D. Searle & Co., 375 F.3d 1303, 1309 (Fed. Cir. 2004) (Rader, J., dissenting from denial of en banc) (arguing for a reexamination of the Federal Circuit's written description doctrine); *see also* Robin C. Feldman, *The Inventor's Contribution*, 2005 UCLA J.L. & TECH. 6, ¶ 34 (2005) (noting that *Enzo II* has left confusion in its wake).

exception to the nucleotide sequence requirement, but it left a trail of uncertainty in its wake.[44]

The Federal Circuit has been unable to resolve the chaos and conflicts because it is looking to science to draw a simple line and provide a concrete solution. Science, however, has no such answers. Pointing to "nucleotide sequences" cannot relieve courts of the responsibility of grappling with difficult questions concerning the nature of the problem addressed by a particular invention, the extent of the advancement created, and the significance of any differences between the advancement and later inventions. These are complex legal questions that must be addressed in the context of the evolution of legal doctrine. When we ignore these questions and turn to science for simple lines of demarcation, it is not surprising that these lines are a failure.

Not only is science ill equipped to answer legal questions, it also is important to remember that scientific lines themselves are constructs. Even the idea of a "gene" is based on an artificial construct. It is a way of conceptualizing a continuous string as if it were broken up into pieces, pieces in which the law now assigns rights.[45] However useful this construct may be, it is still artificial and necessarily glosses over distinctions that may become important as the case law evolves.[46]

---

44 *See* sources cited at note 43.

45 *Cf.* Rebecca Eisenberg at Conference on Biotechnology and Intellectual Property: Current Controversies, March 11, 2005, Stanford Law School (noting that the concept of a gene is based on an artificial notion of dividing DNA according to function).

46 For example, when we talk about a single gene or even the human genome, we are glossing over the fact that significant differences can exist from person to person or between copies of the same gene within a person. Great biological consequences can arise from such small differences, and yet these are differences that we routinely ignore in the legal system. For example, in the *Hoechst* case, the question arose as to whether ownership of one patented

If we simply adopt categories on blind faith without recognizing that they are artificial, we lose the ability to ask whether they fit the legal issues properly as those issues unfold.[47]

Choices made within science are themselves value laden,[48] which makes science less than the neutral arbitrator it might appear. The problem, however, is much more fundamental. In law, we tend to imagine that science is clear and certain. Thus, when we borrow science rules to establish legal rules, we ignore the fact that any choices have been made at all. We cling desperately to the rules as if they are based on solidity and certainty rather than on constructs. Most important, our faith in science blinds us to the questions that a scientific line cannot answer for both the cases in front of us and the cases that will emerge.

---

gene gave rights to its allotype. This was not the question before the court but rather a side issue that had arisen. The court recognized that a difference existed between the patented gene and the one later claimed by the patentee. Going against its own precedent, the court found any differences to be insignificant and moved on. *See* Amgen Inc. v. Hoechst, 314 F.3d at 13331 (affirming the trial courts finding of infringement based on the testimony of patentee's expert testimony that there might be "'minor differences' in applying the method of the disclosed examples (utilizing CHO and COS-1 (monkey) cells) to any vertebrate or mammalian cells, but that those of ordinary skill could 'easily' figure out those differences in methodology").

47 Categorization, although useful, is an artificial construct that cannot transform reality. "Philosophy does not stand outside the world any more than man's brain is outside him because it is not in his stomach." *See* KARL MARX, RHEINISCHE ZEITUNG (July 14, 1882), *reprinted in* 1 KARL MARX & FREDERICK ENGELS, COLLECTED WORKS 195 (1975); *see also* Nussbaum, *supra* note 13, at 1645 (discussing Marx).

48 *See* Harold Kincaid, John Dupré, & Alison Wylie, VALUE-FREE SCIENCE: IDEAS AND ILLUSIONS 10–12 (discussing the nature and effect of values on scientific inquiry); Kristin Shrader-Frechette, *Scientific Progress and Models of Justification: A Case in Hydrogeology, in* STEVEN L. GOLDMAN, SCIENCE, TECHNOLOGY AND SOCIAL PROGRESS 198 (building a theoretical construct on the conclusion that science is "unalterably value-laden").

One could argue that some of the problems with borrowing science rules reflect problems with adopting rules in general. After all, adopting any type of rule rather than a standard gives courts less flexibility. Science rules, however, create different dimensions of the problem. When courts adopt ordinary rules, those rules can be shaped and changed as new cases illuminate the contours of the doctrines. When courts adopt science rules, grafting them onto legal doctrines, the legal system can easily become fixated on those rules. We do not understand the subtleties of the underlying science, and we tend to endow it with mythical powers. As a result, we fail to engage in the natural evolution and adaptation of the resulting doctrines. Thus, the issue is not whether we choose a rule as opposed to a standard. Rather, the issue is where does the rule come from and can it properly evolve.

"A truth that reigns without checks and balances is a tyrant."[49] Feyerabend made this observation some time ago in criticizing the power that science holds over society in general. Although Feyerabend's attacks on science are unnecessarily harsh, the observation above is a useful one for the legal system.[50] When we allow science to reign supreme, we put at risk the careful unfolding of legal doctrine that is at the heart of our legal system.

---

49 P.K. Feyerabend, *How to Defend Society Against Science*, *in* INTRODUCTORY READINGS IN THE PHILOSOPHY OF SCIENCE 56 (E.D. Klemke et al. eds., 1998) [hereinafter KLEMKE].

50 For example, Feyerabend rails "most scientists today are devoid of ideas, full of fear, intent on producing some paltry result so that they can add to the flood of inane papers that now constitutes 'scientific progress' in many areas." *See* Feyerabend, *supra* note 50, at 56*; see also* Paul R. Thagard, *Why Astrology Is a Pseudoscience,* in 1 PROCEEDINGS OF THE PHILOSOPHY OF SCIENCE ASSOCIATION 223, 223 (1978) (referring to Feyerabendian anarchists).

CHAPTER III

Externalization in Modern Law

The prior chapter described how modern courts try to incorporate science into law, crafting legal rules based on scientific lines of demarcation. Rather than trying to incorporate science into rules of law, however, some courts and scholars simply defer to scientists and other experts, granting them the power to resolve uncomfortable legal issues. As described above, we trust in science to provide answers for us or, at the very least, we reassure ourselves that those who have learned how to engage in objective and reliable scientific methodology will have the clarity and objectivity to resolve our legal dilemmas as well.

The legal system is not alone in its tendency to endow scientists with authority to decide all manner of questions. The historian George Sarton describes a similar phenomenon in explaining the authority that Aristotle gained through publication of his immense treatises, known collectively as the Organon.

> There is no doubt that [Aristotle's] immense prestige and excessive authority in the medieval times and later was largely due to his creation of the Organon. . . . that work had the dual effect of discouraging some readers and of increasing their superstitious reverence for the author. In modern times we have frequently witnessed the same kind of paradoxical spectacle. People who were flabbergasted by the (to them) incomprehensible writings of a mathematician accepted the soundness of his philosophic views with incredible passivity. They seemed to think that because they could not understand his mathematics they need not try to understand his philosophy. The creator of the Organon became naturally a master of all knowledge.[51]

Those who can master what we cannot understand gain the authority to resolve what we cannot face.

Outsourcing legal dilemmas to science reflects a lack of faith in the legal system. In fact, some legal actors are quite explicit in their view of law's shortcomings in the face of superior scientific expertise.[52] According to one scholar, for example, one cannot assume that a judge and jury are ever competent to assess human behavior unaided by scientific testimony, given that assessments of human behavior may be based on prejudice.[53]

Our quest for experts to save us from law's dilemmas can lead us to find experts everywhere around us. We run the

---

51 *See* GEORGE SARTON, A HISTORY OF SCIENCE 500 (1952).

52 *See* SHEILA JASANOFF, SCIENCE AT THE BAR: LAW, SCIENCE, AND TECHNOLOGY IN AMERICA xiii–xiv (Harvard 1995) (observing the view of law that conceives of scientific validity as a precondition for rendering legal justice.)

53 *See* Fiona E. Raitt, *A New Criterion for the Admissibility of Scientific Evidence: The Metamorphosis of Helpfulness, in* LAW AND SCIENCE: CURRENT LEGAL ISSUES VOL. 1, 165 (Helen Reece ed., Oxford University Press 1998) (observing that the justification for excluding behavioral science research from evidence ignore "the (human) tendency towards bias, prejudice, and partiality"); *see also* REECE, *supra* note 53, at xi (describing scholar Fiona Raitt).

risk of constructing as expertise any type of information that is not law or common sense.[54] The problems inherent in deferring to experts, however, manifest themselves even where the expertise is clear.

A. ENVIRONMENTAL REGULATION

For example, the instinct to defer to science is in full view in a 2006 Supreme Court case concerning property rights and environmental regulations. In *Rapanos v. U.S.*,[55] the Supreme Court considered whether federal agencies had exceeded the jurisdiction Congress granted them in the Clean Water Act. The Act grants jurisdiction over certain issues related to "navigable waters."[56] In particular, the case addressed whether Congress intended the term "navigable waters" to extend to wetlands not adjacent to any waters that are actually navigable.

While acknowledging that the term "navigable waters" as used in the Act reaches beyond the traditional notion of capable of navigation,[57] some justices complained that the agencies had stretched the definition "beyond parody."[58]

---

54 Michael King & Felicity Kaganas, *The Risks and Dangers of Experts in Court*, *in* REECE, *supra* note 53, at 221–22.

55 Rapanos v. U.S., 547 U.S. 715 (2006).

56 *See id.* at 730.

57 *See id.*

58 *See id.* at 733; *see also id.* at 721 (noting that the agency had interpreted its jurisdiction to include normally dry land features such as roadside ditches, arroyos, or areas that are connected to water by flooding once every 100 years); *see also id.* at 781 (Kennedy, J. concurring in result) (noting that the standard adopted by the agencies seems to leave wide room for regulation of drains, ditches, and streams remote from any navigable-in-fact water and carrying only minor water-volumes towards).

The case reflected a long struggle in which the relevant federal agencies had attempted to define their jurisdiction under the Act as reaching to the

The case reflected a long struggle in which the relevant federal agencies had attempted to define their jurisdiction under the Act as reaching to the full extent of Congress's power to regulate, and the Supreme Court had rejected such an expansive interpretation.

A sharply divided Supreme Court failed to produce a majority opinion. Four Justices joined a plurality opinion, with one of the four filing an additional concurring opinion. A fifth, Justice Kennedy, concurred only in the result. The other four justices joined in a dissenting opinion, with one filing an additional dissent.

Faced with a contentious issue and a clearly divided court, Justice Kennedy attempted to smooth the waters by offering an alternative solution. Justice Kennedy suggested that the proper approach would be to allow the agencies to determine on a case-by-case basis whether the wetlands at issue are likely to play an important role in the integrity of an aquatic system that includes navigable waters as traditionally understood.[59]

Justice Kennedy's test is an inspired compromise, but it begs the question in the case. The test may indeed tell us whether particular wetlands have a sufficient connection to waters involved in interstate commerce so that Congress has the power to regulate them. It cannot, however, tell us whether Congress *intended* to regulate them. There is something comfortable and familiar about Justice Kennedy's test. Let the experts at the agencies parse through the hydrologic interconnections of various parts of the water system and

---

full extent of Congress's power to regulate, and the Supreme Court had rejected such an expansive interpretation. *See id.* at 757–58 (Roberts, J. concurring).

59 *See id.* at 759 (Kennedy, J. concurring in result).

the extent to which these parts relate to traditionally navigable waters. Science will show us the way.

Deferring to science, however, cannot solve the relevant legal question, although it can produce a wealth of impressive sounding information. Science can help determine whether things are the same and can identify the ways in which they differ. Science cannot, however, tell us whether that sameness matters from a legal perspective.

B. ANTITRUST

The prior sections have described modern efforts to bring science into law by importing scientific lines of demarcation as legal rules. They have also described efforts to export law's difficult questions by deferring legal questions to scientific experts. Some modern areas of law display both of these trends, importing science into law as well as exporting laws questions to scientific experts. Consider modern debates in the application of economics to antitrust law.

The pervasive influence of economics in modern legal thought is undeniable. As Richard Epstein has noted, the magnitude of the law and economics revolution is hard to explain because the analysis of most private law subjects today is so heavily influenced by economic thought that scholars could not proceed without it.[60] This is particularly true of antitrust law, where it is difficult to imagine examining a firm's behavior under the antitrust laws without applying sophisticated economic analysis.

With law's wholesale adoption of economics into the antitrust arena, we consistently run into one simple problem: Courts can't do it, particularly where the practice at

60 *See* Richard A. Epstein, *Law and Economics: Its Glorious Past and Cloudy Future*, 54 CHICAGO L. REV. 1167, 1167, 1173 (1997).

issue must be evaluated over time and in complex market settings.[61] In fact, one prominent law and economics scholar, Frank Easterbrook, has argued that courts are unable to apply even basic economic analysis in individual cases.[62]

> The inquiry mandated by the Rule of Reason is whether the challenged agreement is one that promotes competition or one that suppresses competition. . . . It must consider the facts peculiar to the business to which the restraint is applied; its condition before and after the restraint was imposed; the nature of the restraint and its effect, actual or probable. The history of the restraint, the evil believed to exist, the reason for adopting the particular remedy, the purpose or end sought to be achieved are all relevant facts. These formulations are empty. Judges and justices rightly protest that courts cannot make these judgments.[63]

---

61 *See e.g.*, Barry Wright Corp. v. ITT Grinnell Corp., 724 F.2d 227, 234 (1st Cir. 1983) (arguing that law cannot replicate economics); *see also* United States v. Topco Assocs., 405 U.S. 596, 609, 611–12 (1972) (footnote omitted) (arguing that courts are of limited utility in examining difficult economic problems, ill equipped and ill suited to analyze, interpret, and evaluate the myriad of competing interests and the endless data that would surely be brought to bear on such decisions); A. Douglas Melamed, *Exclusionary Conduct Under the Antitrust Laws: Balancing, Sacrifice, and Refusals to Deal*, 20 BERKELEY TECH. L.J. 1247, 1250 (2005) (noting that some critics of certain modern antitrust cases complain that antitrust courts either cannot be counted on to get difficult economic and technical issues right); *cf.* SI Handling Systems v. Heisley, 753 F.2d 1244, 1266–69 (3d Cir. 1985) (Adams, J. concurring) (noting in a trade secret case, "it would seem that a court cannot act as a pure engineer or scientist").

62 *See* Frank H. Easterbrook, *The Limits of Antitrust*, 63 TEX. L. REV. 1, 11 (1984).

63 *See id.* at 11–12; *see also id.* at 11 (arguing that it is fantastic to suppose that judges and juries could conduct a full inquiry into the economic costs and benefits of a particular business practice in the setting in which it has been used).

Easterbrook, himself a judge, is echoing complaints heard from other corners of the bench.[64] He argues that while an economist at least has the ability to approach the evaluation of unfamiliar business practices, a judge today does not.[65] The problem is partly one of capacity. Judges, juries, lawyers, and even most staff members at the Federal Trade Commission and the Department of Justice are not economists. By crafting antitrust rules grounded in economic analyses, however, we ask all these parties to engage in sophisticated economics. It is not surprising that the results are disappointing. As Justice Breyer wrote in an antitrust opinion prior to joining the Supreme Court:

> [W]hile technical economic discussion helps to inform the antitrust laws, those laws cannot precisely replicate the economists' (sometimes conflicting) thinking. For, unlike economics, law is an administrative system the effects of which depend upon the content of rules and precedents only as they are applied by judges and juries and by lawyers advising their clients. Rules that seek to embody every economic complexity and qualification may well, through the vagaries of administration, prove counter-productive, undercutting the very economic ends they seek to serve.[66]

Lack of capacity, however, is not the only reason economic analyses yield disappointing results in a legal setting. It is also a problem of the forum. There is a difference between the simplifying assumptions that can be applied in an economist's pristine lab and the messy complexity that emerges in an individual case. This is particularly true when a real firm's behavior must be evaluated over time, among

64 *See* sources cited *supra* note 61 (citing *Topco* and *Barry Wright Corp.*).

65 *See* Easterbrook, *supra* note 62, at 11.

66 Barry Wright Corp. v. ITT Grinnell Corp., 724 F.2d 227, 234 (1st Cir. 1983) (citations omitted).

multiple products, and within markets that are far from idealized and populated with executives who have imperfect information. The reality of any individual case makes economic rules difficulty to apply in a manageable form.

Nevertheless, having imported economic analysis, what is to be done? For some, the answer lies in limiting law's domain. Courts should act only in certain categories of cases that involve application of more simplistic models.[67]

---

67 *See* Oliver E. Williamson, *Delimiting Antitrust*, 76 Geo. L.J. 271, 277–79 (1987) (identifying a modern school of antitrust thought that believes courts have limited ability to deal with tradeoffs or more sophisticated economic reasoning, that these conditions are unchanging, and that simpler legal rules should be applied); *see also* Phillip Areeda & Donald F. Turner, *Scherer on Predatory Pricing: A Reply*, 89 HARV. L. REV. 891, 897 (1976) (noting that long-run possibilities should be disregarded as too indeterminate and unsuitable for any administrative rules that could give them recognition); Richard A. Posner, *Antitrust Policy and the Supreme Court: An Analysis of the Restricted Distribution, Horizontal Merger, and Potential Competition Decisions*, 75 COLUMBIA L. REV. 282, 326 (1975) (arguing that one factor in the failure of the Court to create a "coherent and rational body of antitrust doctrine . . . [was that] antitrust may be too difficult a body of law to be consigned to nonspecialists for its development and application"); Barbara Ann White, *Choosing Among Antitrust Liability Standards Under Incomplete Information: Assessments of and Aversions to the Risk of Being Wrong*, 20 BERKELEY TECH. L.J. 1173, 1173 (2005) (describing McGowan's view that in the realm of reality, courts must make decisions under conditions of imperfect information, not only as to the anticompetitiveness of the scrutinized conduct but also as to the impact of their decisions, since incomplete information implies a risk that whatever the court decides, the decision is wrong); *see* Michael S. Jacobs, *The New Sophistication in Antitrust*, 79 MINN. L. REV. 1, 38 (1994) (noting that Chicago scholars doubt the judiciary's ability to use complicated strategic models and to analyze their antitrust implications); *see also* David McGowan, *Between Logic and Experience: Error Costs and United States v. Microsoft Corp.*, 20 BERKELEY TECH. L.J. 1185, 1186 (2005).

Chicago school scholars like Melamed and Werden express some faith in the courts' ability to engage in a degree of measurement, although they would limit measurement to more basic economic analyses. *See* Melamed, *supra* note 61, at 1255–56 (advocating the "profit sacrifice" test which compares

This approach, of course, has the happy circumstance of giving preference to one school of economic thought over another. It is the Chicago school's theories that tend to be based on the streamlined economic models and the post-Chicago school's theories that require consideration of more complex factors.[68] The two lead to drastically different implications for when courts should intervene in business behavior.

For others, the solution is to establish filters, groupings of cases for which the court will ignore unfamiliar business practices rather than engaging in a detailed analysis of the effects of those practices in the particular case.[69] The notion that streamlined legal categories can be developed from insights that we gain across time makes sense. Nevertheless, one must ask how we derive those filters. If we are not using

---

the benefits and costs to the defendants of the conduct in question); Gregory J. Werden, *Principle and Execution: The "No Economic Sense" Test for Exclusionary Conduct*, 31 Iowa J. Corp. L. 293, 303 (advocating the "no economic sense" rule which measures whether the conduct likely would have been profitable under the assumption that a monopoly was not created because the existing competitors were not excluded). As described below however, scholars like Frank Easterbrook seem to be saying that courts cannot really handle even basic economic analyses like the Rule of Reason so let's just do it as infrequently as possible by applying filters. *See* Easterbrook, *supra* note 62.

68 *See, e.g.*, Robin C. Feldman, *Defensive Leveraging in Antitrust*, 87 Georgetown L.J. 2079, 2084–88 (1999) (explaining Chicago and post-Chicago school perspectives); Herbert Hovenkamp, *Antitrust Policy after Chicago*, 84 Mich. L. Rev. 213, 224–25 (1985) [hereinafter Hovenkamp, *Antitrust*] (noting that the simplicity of the law and economics models made it much easier to declare behavior such as product differentiation harmless whereas this behavior have been considered suspect previously); Jacobs, *supra* note 67, at 37 (noting that post-Chicago scholars have used industrial organization and game theory approaches to develop models of strategic behavior and argue that the broad generalizations of price theory may be inappropriate when individual firms act strategically).

69 *See* Easterbrook, *supra* note 62, at 14–39 (describing proposed filters).

the experience of examining individual cases to develop the categories, there is a risk that the categories are simply dictated by economists, perhaps even a particular group of economists or a particular period of economic theory. In that case, judges would move from acting as economists to simply deferring to economists.

The instinct to defer to economists does not reside only with Chicago scholars. For example, Oliver Williamson, a post-Chicago scholar has suggested that antitrust rules could contain the following introductory statement: "Temporarily, pending further economic analysis and deeper understanding of the economic institutions and practices in question, the legal rule for dealing with this class of cases will be. . . ."[70] Again, the question is not whether new insights can be developed over time upon which antitrust law may rely. The question is whether economists are the sole mechanism of development of those insights, which the courts then passively accept, or whether the courts play an active role in developing and shaping those insights that become adapted as legal rules.

Deferring to economists would be an abdication to science rather than an appreciation of what science can bring to judicial decision making. Even that abdication might seem like blessed relief, however, if it brought clarity and certainty to a difficult area of law. The proposed filters and simplified models, however, are value laden and subject to dispute even among those who agree that filters should be adopted.[71] Reaching for the social science of economics cannot bring the rationality and neutrality that we crave.

---

70 *See* Williamson, *supra* note 67, at 279.

71 Compare Melamed, *supra* note 67 (advocating the "profit sacrifice test") with Werden, *supra* note 67 (advocating the "no economic sense rule").

There has always been a trade-off in law between precision and simplicity. In this case, however, the plea for simplicity arises because science is considered too complex to apply in a judicial or administrative setting. We should not ask, "What is wrong with those courts and agencies that they cannot apply economics?" Rather, we should ask, "What is wrong with this system of measurement for the judicial setting?"

This is not to suggest that antitrust should proceed without the benefit of economic insights. Economics, as the core of antitrust, is here to stay, and it will continue to play an important role in encouraging the development of rational utilitarian frameworks for this area of law. Given the limits of economics in a judicial setting, however, the question is where we should turn in our efforts to make those economic insights useful in a judicial setting.[72]

Wherever we turn, we must avoid a fixation with measurement. There may be things we can measure with precision and things we cannot measure, but law is not necessarily about measurement. For example, we may not the able to precisely measure the size of a particular market that would

72 In an early case at the intersection of patent and antitrust, the Supreme Court refused to rely on antirust rules for a finding of patent misuse. The Court suggested, however, that the logic of why certain behaviors raised concerns in an antitrust context would give further insight into why those behaviors might be of concern in the context of patent policy. The rules, however, would have to be based on patent law. *See* Motion Picture Patents Co. v. Universal Film Mfg., 243 U.S. 502, 514, 517–18 (1917); *see also* Robin C. Feldman, *The Insufficiency of Antitrust Analysis for Patent Misuse*, 55 HASTINGS L.J. 399, 407 (2003) (describing the development of patent misuse). Antitrust insights might inspire the formation of patent misuse rules, as long as the formation of those rules rests on the logic of patent policy. Similarly, economic insights may inspire antitrust rules, as long as antirust rules rest on the logic of legal policy and are not simply economic formulas substituted for legal rules.

have developed but for strategic anticompetitive behavior. Nevertheless, we might still choose to respond to a firm that repeatedly suppresses the emergence of any future technology that might erode its monopoly power. The impossibility of the task should not matter if the task is not the essence of the enterprise.

Most important, the deeper challenge is to recognize a consistent pattern of behavior in the legal system. We begin with an overexuberant embrace of a science as the solution to our difficult legal problems. Over time, the limitations of that science in the legal realm become apparent. This pattern should suggest a problem with the rubric, an indication of the way in which science cannot assist law. Instead, it is interpreted as a weakness of law, a point at which law must cease to operate and lawyers must defer to experts. Worse yet, the experience is simply forgotten and played out repeatedly at other times and in other segments of the legal realm.

CHAPTER IV

The Repetitions of History

In modern law, one can see many examples in which courts and scholars reach for science when faced with uncomfortable legal dilemmas. We internalize science by borrowing science rules for legal doctrines or we externalize our problems by giving scientists and other experts the power to make legal decisions. Our deference to these pillars of neutral rationality is supposed to bring clarity, certainty, and a resolution that all can respect. The strategy continually fails, however, leaving as much chaos, confusion, and disagreement as before.

Law's fascination with science reaches back hundreds of years into American legal history. At times, it takes the form of trying to make law into a science or to make lawyers into scientists. At times, it takes the form of simply deferring to scientific fields. Throughout this history, however, the pattern of behavior reflects our doubts about whether law is capable of resolving difficult issues and our eternal hope that science can do it better. The notion of what constitutes science and what it would mean to make law more scientific varies across time and among scholars.[73] What does not vary is our abiding faith that science will rescue us from the discomfort and uncertainties of law and our continual disappointment.

A. LEGAL THEORY MOVEMENTS

During the first half of the nineteenth century, a number of American legal scholars advocated approaching law as a science.[74] To some, the notion meant conceptualizing law as an organized system, rather than a loose collection of precedents. To others, it meant approaching law as an outgrowth of moral science. To still others, it meant law as analogous to natural science. The latter group, in particular, argued that the study of law should follow the methods and reasoning of scientific investigation applied in the natural sciences at the

73 *See* Howard Schweber, The "Science" of Legal Science: The Model of the Natural Sciences in Nineteenth Century American Legal Education, 17 LAW & HIST. REV. 421, 421–22 (1999) (comparing differing views of nineteenth century legal scholars concerning the meaning of law as a science); *see also* Charles Barzun, *Common Sense and Legal Science*, 90 VA. L. REV. 1051, 1055 (discussing nineteenth-century philosopher's belief "that they could discover natural legal principles just as Newton had discovered the laws of nature."); Harold Berman & Charles J. Reid Jr., *The Transformation of English Legal Science: From Hale to Blackstone*, 45 EMORY L.J. 437, 441 (noting that "legal science may refer not only to a systematic body of knowledge about law generated by legal scholars . . . [but] also to a systematic body of knowledge generated by the law itself, defining its functions and the ways in which it operates.").

74 *See id.* at 422 (explaining the differing views described below). Yearnings to make law into a science did not originate in American legal history. Other traces can be found in early Roman law and in later European Law. *See* PETER STEIN, ROMAN LAW IN EUROPEAN HISTORY 79, 99 (1999). The focus of this piece, however, is on the repeated appearance of this theme in American legal history.

time. Observations of law, like the observations of nature, should trace the origins and developmental paths of legal doctrine to identify the enduring and stable principles.

As Bishop explained, laws that govern men in society, "operate steadily, constantly, and uniformly; as does the law which draws the rivulet steadily and constantly downstream . . . [a]nd as a particular motion of the stream is not the law of the stream, but only evidence of the law."[75] Therefore, like the natural science taxonomists of the time, legal scholars should engage in an exhaustive and exact study of laws and cases to discover the universal and natural governing principles of human affairs.[76] These natural governing principles were supposed to be universally acceptable and understandable to all through "common sense," given that everyone was presumed to share the experience of perception and that everyone's perceptions were presumed to be consistent.[77] This movement represented reconceptualizing law as analogous to the natural science movement of the time.

---

75 Joel P. Bishop, The First Book of the Law 47 (1868); *see also* David Dudley Field, *Magnitude and Importance of Legal Science, in* Speeches, Arguments, and Miscellaneous Papers of David Dudley Field 526–27 (A.P. Sprague, ed. 1884) (analogizing the proper study of law to descending from a mountaintop in order to understand the landscape in its vast, varied, and finite details), *available at* www.heinonline.org.

76 *See* Schweber, *supra* note 73, at 450–51; *see also* Daniel Mays, *Whether Law is a Science: An Introductory Lecture Delivered to the Law Class of Transylvania University, on the 8th of November, 1832*, 369 (1832) (arguing that "[C]ases are useful; but their greatest use is, that they serve to illustrate principles. If they are read and not resolved into elementary principles, the profit of the reading is not worth the time it occupies"), *available at* www.heinonline.orgwww.heinonline.org.

77 *See* Schweber, *supra* note 73, at 442–45 (describing the influence of Scottish Common Sense theory on Baconism and the influence of Baconism on nineteenth century American legal thought).

American legal scholars were not alone in the effort to improve law by treating it as a science. In British jurisprudence, both Jeremy Bentham and William Blackstone advocated such a path in the late eighteenth and early nineteenth centuries. Although their philosophies differed, they were united in their passion for scientific methodology and reasoning through statistical study.[78] Blackstone, for example, described law as "a science which distinguishes the criteria of right and wrong" and advocated a deductive system of legal reasoning that would incorporate natural law principles.[79] Similarly, Bentham described his own piece, *The Principles of Morals and Legislation*, as analogous to a math treatise.[80]

It is important to remember that not all legal scholars who described law in the language of science had the natural sciences in mind. Some scholars during this period used the word "experimental" to mean simply based on experience and "science" to mean any system of knowledge.[81] Thus, when British theorist Thomas Macaulay wrote in 1833 that the "science of government is an experimental science," he was not thinking of laboratory investigations and physics but of organized thought founded on solid experience

---

78 *See* John McEldowney, *The Environment, Science, and Law, in* REECE, *supra* note 53, at 111.

79 Albert W. Alschuler, *Rediscovering Blackstone*, 145 U. PA. L. REV. 1, 55 (1996); *see also* 1 WILLIAM BLACKSTONE, COMMENTARIES 27; McEldowney, *supra* note 78, at 112.

80 *See* M. LOBBAN, THE COMMON LAW AND ENGLISH JURISPRUDENCE 1760–1850, 155 (1991); *see also* Charles L. Barzun, Note, *Common Sense and Legal Science*, 90 VA. L. REV. 1051, 1079–88 (2004) (examining Gulian Verplanck's *Essay on the Doctrine of Contracts* as an example of inductive reasoning used to derive principles of contract law from personal moral intuition legal philosophy in the nineteenth century).

81 *See* BOSTON STUDIES, *supra* note 4, at 7.

revealed through the historical record.[82] As described above, the notion of law as a science has differing meanings for differing philosophers of the time, including the notion of approaching law as a natural science.[83]

Reconceptualizing law as analogous to natural science failed to bring clarity or universal agreement concerning legal principles for American legal scholars of this period. Among its many problems, scholars following the natural science approach argued strongly in favor of slavery during the Civil War. When those views were discredited in the post-Civil War era, the theoretical approaches were discredited as well.[84]

Law's love affair with the natural sciences flourished again in the 1870s and found an institutional home with the arrival of Christopher Columbus Langdell as the dean of Harvard Law School.[85] Langdell certainly was not the first to conceptualize law as legal science, but his efforts popularized the notion, leaving an enduring stamp on American legal education.[86]

Langdell wanted to transform legal education from the teaching of a craft into a scholarly endeavor worthy of a

82 *See id.* at 207–08.

83 *See supra* text accompanying notes 74–77.

84 *See* Schweber, *supra* note 73 at 455–56; *see also* Michael V. Hernandez, *A Flawed Foundation: Christianity's Loss of Preeminent Influence on American Law*, 56 RUTGERS L. REV. 625, 709 (noting that "a biblical worldview, anti-Darwinism, and natural science were direct casualties of the Civil War.").

85 *See* Grey, *Langdell's Orthodoxy*, *supra* note 13, at 1.

86 *See* ROGER BERKOWITZ, THE GIFT OF SCIENCE: LEIBNIZ AND THE MODERN LEGAL TRADITION, 121 (2005) (noting that Langdell should be remembered for his popularization efforts rather than his innovativeness or originality and that he was but a link in a chain of tradition stretching back two centuries and across the Atlantic).

place of honor among the great universities of the nation.[87] To bring legal education into this fold, Langdell suggested that using scientific methods, scholars could identify fundamental principles and axioms which lawyers could apply to reach the proper solution to any legal problem.[88] Cases would be the data set for the scientific inquiry, and from this data set, one could derive the fundamental principles of private law.[89]

This legal science was not a deductive science, like mathematics, in which a series of true statements can be used to derive another statement that is necessarily true.[90] Rather, it was more an inductive field science, like botany, in which one uses a series of examples from the available specimens to derive general principles.[91]

The notion of law as a clear and structured science also offered relief from the bewildering array of issues emerging in the late 1800s. With industrialization, the range and complexity of the economic transactions regulated by case

---

87 *See* Martha C. Nussbaum, *The Use and Abuse of Philosophy in Legal Education*, 45 STAN. L. REV. 1627, 1629 (1993).

88 *See* Bix, *Positively Positivism*, *supra* note 13, at 892; Grey, *Langdell's Orthodoxy*, *supra* note 13, at 5. Publications at the time included THE SCIENCE OF LAW (1874) (containing a foldout chart ofThe Scheme of a Body of Laws for the Modern State); S. AMOS, THE SCIENCE OF LAW 119 (1874) (noting that law is composed of elements as permanent add universal as the elements of human nature itself); and E. CAMPBELL, THE SCIENCE OF LAW, ACCORDING TO THE AMERICAN THEORY OF GOVERNMENT 6 (arguing that "the principles of justice are a definite body of immutable principles, and hence constitute a true science"). *See* Veilleux, *supra* note 13, at nn.44–48 and accompanying text (describing these and other scholarly publications of the late 1800s).

89 *See* Veilleux, *supra* note 13, at 1975.

90 *See* Bix, *supra* note 13, at 892 (noting that Langdell's analyses were not deductive); *see also* Philip Kitcher, *Believing Where We Cannot Prove, in* KLEMKE, *supra* note 49, at 81–82 (describing deductive reasoning).

91 *See* Bix, *supra* note 13, at 892; SIMON BLACKBURN, THE OXFORD DICTIONARY OF PHILOSOPHY 192 (1994) (describing inductive reasoning).

law expanded dramatically.[92] This change put tremendous pressure on a legal system that frequently relied on a judge's understanding of long-standing customs.[93] One could not rely on custom in the face of rapid changes in the nature and complexity of societal interactions. Law, conceptualized as a structured science, offered great appeal in times of turmoil and increasing complexity.[94]

The legal system, however, stubbornly refused to conform to any notion of a rational science. Its treasured data bank of cases failed to reveal a clear structure of higher order principles branching into ancillary rules, despite valiant efforts at analysis.[95] In particular, critics pointed out that cases frequently contradicted each other and any apparent guiding principles.[96] Later attempts to organize the law into

---

92 *See* Lawrence Lessig, *Fidelity and Constraint*, 65 FORDHAM L. REV., 1365, 1403 (1997).

93 *See id*; *cf.* McEldowney, *supra* note 78, at 111 (noting that the English common law tradition, which was based on providing suitable remedies in an individual case, offered only solutions that were narrowly defined and limited by procedure and form).

94 *See* CHRISTOPHER C. LANGDELL, A SELECTION OF CASES ON THE LAW OF CONTRACTS viii–ix (1871) *quoted in* Stephen M. Feldman, *The New Metaphysics: The Interpretive Turn in Jurisprudence*, 76 IOWA L. REV. 661, 661 n.5 (1991) (arguing that "[l]aw, considered as a science, consists of certain principles or doctrines. . . . If these doctrines could be so classified and arranged that each should be found in its proper place, and nowhere else, they would cease to be formidable from their number.").

95 As Austin noted in his lectures on jurisprudence, "[i]deal completeness and correctness . . . is not attainable . . . though the system had been built and ordered with matchless solicitude and skill." *See* 2 AUSTIN, LECTURES ON JURISPRUDENCE 997–98 (5th ed. 1885).

96 *See* Felix S. Cohen, *Transcendental Nonsense and the Functional Approach*, 35 COLUM. LAW. REV. 809 (1935) (noting that the practice of legal reasoning often ignores facts and practical consequences and rather is based on the manipulation of legal concepts in certain approved ways.); *see also* KELMAN, *supra* note 13, at 46 (noting that one of the most entertaining sports that critics of Langdellian legal science engaged in was to tweak their

restatements and treatises produced great and complex compendiums lacking the simple clarity suggested in the notion of law as a science.[97]

As law failed to live up to the notion of an inductive natural science, other schools of thought emerged in opposition. For example, the progressives, including scholars like Holmes, Pound, and Cardozo, suggested that legislators were the main instruments of law rather than judges and argued that law could be understood as policies rather than rules. Many progressives felt that although an exact, internal legal science was a chimera, law could be reconstructed as a policy science around social science. Law would not be a deductive science but a science of informed experiment in which appropriate legal actors could use social science to guide them to various policies that could be tested and refined across time.

In this context, progressives urged that legislators and experts at administrative agencies should apply social science as a guide to the proper policies. Judges, too, could apply social science to fill in the gaps left by legislators in their quest for the right policies, although their role should be limited. Thus, law itself might not be a physical science, but legal actors could operate like social scientists, engaging in a type of informed experiment to find their way to an enlightened path for society.

---

treatise-writing, rule-collecting Formalist forbearers for announcing that they had discovered legal rules that were, on inspection, utterly vacuous and question begging).

97 *See* Grey, *Modern American Legal Thought, supra* note 13, at 500 (describing the collaboration between Langdellians in writing the first Restatements, and noting the legal realist critiques of these Restatements as well as the treatises of the era); Arnold, Institute Priests and Yale Observers—A Reply to Dean Goodrich, 84 U. Pa. L. Rev. 811, 820 (1936) (criticizing restatements).

Tucked into the progressive perspective as well as that of Langdellian legal science, one sees a valiant effort to find a way to conceptualize law so that it can be understood as necessarily moving forward, ever closer to what is right and what is good. It is an effort one sees in a variety of legal movements, as well as individual legal scholars even to the present. Steven Winter, for example, explains that the transformative potential of law and legal metaphor ensure that "the violent apparatus of the legal state is never immune from real progress in creating a more tolerant and free society."[98] These efforts reflect a craving for finding a way to define law as necessarily evolutionary toward the good, an effort that is often challenged by the criticisms of the following legal movements.

In the case of the progressives it was the legal realists who followed quickly on their heels, leveling sharp criticisms.[99] Legal realists argued that the progressives' cherished policy science was no more clear or predictable than the rules and axioms of a natural science approach. Legal realists believed that laws and precedents were indeterminate, capable of a myriad of interpretations. Words, according to the legal realists, are inherently open ended.[100] Moreover, conflicting rules

98 *See* REECE, *supra* note 53, at 13.

99 *See* Stephen M. Feldman, *The Transformation of an Academic Discipline: Law Professors in the Past and Future (or Toy Story Too)*, 54 J. LEGAL EDUC. 471, 482–83 (2004) (noting the development of progressive legal theories such as those of Roscoe Pound around the turn of the twentieth century, and the emergence of Legal Realism in the 1920s and 1930s).

100 *See* Jerome Frank, *Words and Music: Some Remarks on Statutory Interpretation*, 47 COLUM. L. REV. 1259, 1263 (1947) (noting that people's annoyance with the way judges sometimes interpret apparently simple statutory language is based on the false assumption that each verbal symbol refers to one and only one specific subject, and a denial of the wide range of ambiguities a word may have that can only be resolved through consideration of context and background); Felix Frankfurter, *Some Reflections on the Reading of*

frequently cover the factual circumstance, and no autonomous mechanical rules can clearly govern the conflict.[101] Legal realists thought that judges inevitably responded to their own perspectives and prejudices.[102] The process of law, according to the legal realists, involved intuitive dispute resolution in light of unconsciously absorbed custom.[103]

Law's interrelation with science endured for the realists, but in a slightly different form. For the realists, judges and legal scholars could use social science to better understand themselves.[104] Studying themselves would help scholars reveal

---

Statutes, 47 COLUM. L. REV. 527, 528 (1947) (noting that words are symbols of meaning, but unlike mathematical symbols, the phrasing of a document, especially a complicated enactment, seldom attains more than approximate precision); *see also* KELMAN, *supra* note 13, at 12–13 (describing the Realists).

101 *See* KELMAN, *supra* note 13, at 45; Roscoe Pound, *Mechanical Jurisprudence*, 8 COLUM. L. REV. 605, 606–14 (1908) (warning against the cyclical petrifaction of the common law where longstanding legal doctrines are unexamined and mechanically applied, and ultimately fail to respond to the human conditions and complexities of present day life).

102 *See, e.g.*, Karl N. Llewellyn, *"Law and the Modern Mind": A Symposium*, 31 COLUM. L. REV 82, 83 (1931) (reviewing JEROME FRANK, LAW AND THE MODERN MIND (1930)) (contrasting the myth that the great bulk of a judge's work is "mere routine application of accepted rules" with the reality that no different from witnesses, a judge's perception of "the facts" varies according to temperament and circumstance, and a judge's selection, stress, and arrangement of "the facts" can make the most peculiar case look routine).

103 *See* Grey, *Langdell's Orthodoxy*, *supra* note 13, at 503.

104 *See* Karl N. Llewellyn, *Some Realism about Realism: Responding to Dean Pound*, 44 HARVARD LAW REVIEW 1222 (1931) (serving as a classic example of social scientific self-examination through the employment of statistical, textual analysis upon the then-emerging writings of perceived new legal realists in order to discover if indeed a common school of legal realists exists); FRANK, *supra* note 5, at 178–80 (using psychology to explain that the wish for things certain and secure is an infantile, regressive tendency and to advocate that judges recognize that all rules and standards are fictions, to appreciate law's dynamic qualities, and to struggle against the drag of childish nostalgia for the over-secure and serene); *see also* Grey, *Modern American Legal Thought*, *supra* note 13, at 510 (describing the legal realists).

the indeterminate and individualized nature of judging and would help judges better understand and follow their unconscious instincts.[105] Legal actors were still analogous to social scientists but the subject of study was themselves.

The legal realists' faith in social science was also reflected in their devotion to the continued rise of the regulatory state. Both realists and progressives viewed administrative government as the scientific solution to the economic and social crises of the 1920s and 1930s.[106] Judges were viewed as lacking the means, the expertise, and perhaps the will to bring about the changes necessary to keep pace with the tremendous upheavals of the time.[107]

Administrative agencies during this period were given extraordinary discretion in deference to their expertise.[108] This deference was justified on grounds both that agency experts were superior in capacity and that their expertise made them more trustworthy. For example, in describing the need for limited judicial oversight, the Supreme Court commented that an agency "deals with a subject that is highly specialized and so complex as to be the despair of judges"

---

105 *See* Grey, *Modern American Legal Thought, supra* note 13, at 501; *see also* LAURA KALMAN, THE STRANGE CAREER OF LEGAL LIBERALISM 16 (1996) (noting that legal realists debunked the law as an effort to improve it by treating it as a tool of social policy).

106 *See* Reuel E. Schiller, *Reining in the Administrative State: World War II and the Decline of Expert Administration, in* DANIEL R. ERNST & VICTOR JEW, TOTAL WAR AND THE LAW 185, 201 (2002) [hereinafter *Decline of the Expert Administration*].

107 *See* KALMAN, *supra* note 105, at 18.

108 *See* Schiller, *Decline of the Expert Administration, supra* note 106, at 286–88; Reuel E. Schiller, *Enlarging the Administrative Polity: Administrative Law and the Changing Definition of Pluralism 1945–1970*, 53 VAND L. REV. 1389, 1404 (2000) (describing New Deal era judicial deference to administrative agencies) [hereinafter *Changing Definitions*].

and is "better staffed for its task than is the judiciary."[109] In another case, the Court expressed its faith in agency experts by noting that "the training that is required, the comprehensive knowledge which is possessed, guards against accidental abuse of its powers or, if the abuse occurs, to correct it."[110] Thus, expertise would make those at agencies the neutral and dependable arbiters of difficult legal dilemmas.

The legal process school, which began to emerge in the late 1930s in response to legal realism, reinforced faith in the administrative state.[111] If our perspectives are hopelessly clouded and words are inherently open ended, how are we to function as a legal system? Most importantly, if the legal realists were right that rules are subject to infinite interpretations and that perspectives can never be objective, how can law hope to be anything more than the subjective whims of individual judges? What rational domain is left for law?[112]

The legal process school offered one response to such unsettling visions of indeterminacy and unconstrained discretion. Legal process argued that law could function best in the realm of choosing the institution or procedure appropriate for resolving a particular question.[113] Law might not have a monopoly on finding principles that would yield the right answer or on the wise and selfless neutrality that would lead to a universally acceptable result. Nevertheless, legal actors might be particularly skilled at identifying which

---

109 *See* Dobson v. Commissioner, 320 U.S. 242, 245 (1943).

110 *See* Perkins v. Lukens Steel Co., 310 U.S. 113, 127–28 (1940).

111 *See* Bix, *supra* note 13, at 896 (describing the legal process school as a response to legal realism); KALMAN, *supra* note 104, at 19 (discussing the timing of the emergence of the legal process school).

112 *See*, *id.* at 896 (describing discomfort in the wake of the legal realist critique).

113 *See* KELMAN, *supra* note 13, at 6.

institutions and processes could function most appropriately for addressing the question at hand.[114]

Tucked into the legal process perspective was the notion that the legal system has limited competence for addressing some of the issues that come before it. In that terrain, legal actors should simply defer to the experts. This instinct to circumscribe the domain of law by deferring to experts is a theme that echoes in modern manifestations of law and science.

Critics of the legal process school would later suggest that arguments made about one institution can be made for any other institution.[115] From this perspective, similar arguments of bias and lack of access can be leveled at any institution in relation to any particular legal question. Thus, the promise of improving law by evaluating and comparing institutions remained unfulfilled.

In general, law's euphoria over agency expertise, so strong in the 1920s and 30s, soured within a couple of decades. By the 1950s and 60s, Americans had gained experience abroad with the monstrous expressions of administrative power in fascist states as well as experience at home with wartime agencies that more often appeared to be "incompetent bullies" rather than rational, neutral arbiters.[116] Agencies

---

114 *See* Bix, *supra* note 13, at 897; Calabresi, *supra* note 13, at 2143–44 (describing the legal process school using the issue of ownership of body parts); *see also* Schiller, *Changing Definitions, supra* note 108, at 1402 (noting that process theorists such as Bickel, Wechsler, Wellington, Sachs, and Hart, suggested each branch of government undertake tasks for which it is best suited).

115 *See* KELMAN, *supra* note 13, at 190–91 (describing critical legal studies critiques of the legal process school and what he calls the deification of process); *cf.* Edward L. Rubin, *The New Legal Process, The Synthesis of Discourse, and the Microanalysis of Institutions*, 10 HARV. L. REV. 1393, 1400–01 (outlining criticisms by critical legal studies on the legal process school).

116 *See* Schiller, *Decline of the Expert Administration, supra* note 106, at 201.

would remain, along with their powerful influence on the American landscape. Once admitted, the administrative expertise would not be expelled. Nevertheless, the image of an administrative state in which experts would solve the legal system's intractable problems faded.[117]

One cannot examine the interrelation of law and social science without paying homage to the law and economics movement. Law and economics is perhaps the most influential school of thought that has specifically tried to merge law with a particular social science, in this case economics.

Law and economics gained prominence in the 1970s.[118] The elegance and simplicity of law and economics offered great appeal to a legal academic community still reeling from the devastating critiques of the legal realists and the indeterminacy of legal realism.[119] Law and economics can be seen as suggesting a solution to the turmoil that had plagued post-realist legal academics who had been taught that legal rules were essentially no more than policy decisions.[120]

According to law and economics, the proper role of legal actors is to apply the insights of economics, particularly neoclassical price theory, to legal questions in an effort to craft efficient legal rules that create the proper incentives for

---

117 *See generally* Schiller, *Decline of the Expert Administration*, *supra* note 106 (describing the disenchantment with the administrative state and the imposition of due process requirements and court supervision).

118 *See* KELMAN, *supra* note 13, at 114.

119 *See* KELMAN, *supra* note 13, at 118 (noting that the so-called Chicago school of law and economics brought a message of simplicity to an academic and social world in search of simplicity); *see also* Ugo Mattei, *The Rise and Fall of Law and Economics: An Essay for Judge Guido Calabresi*, 64 MD. L. REV. 220, 235 (noting that characteristics such as relative simplicity, political ambiguity, and universality helped fuel the spread of law and economics).

120 *See* KELMAN, *supra* note 13, at 125.

optimal behavior.[121] This will promote satisfaction of the greatest possible level of overall societal wants.[122] For example, law and economics scholarship in tort law has suggested that the goal of tort law and regulation should be to create the proper incentives that will force individuals to internalize the consequences that their decisions inflicted on others, thereby minimizing the divergence between private and social costs.[123]

In one respect, one can think of law and economics as a particular variant of the legal process school. Law and economics scholars treat "the market" as analogous to a separate institution in itself. Legal actors must consider whether the institution of the market is more capable of resolving the problem at hand than courts or administrative agencies.

---

121 *See* Hovenkamp, *Antitrust, supra* note 68, at 224 (noting that an important difference between the neoclassical market efficiency model, used by law and economics scholars, and earlier economic models is that the neoclassical model claims a much greater ability to distinguish between efficient and inefficient policies); Hovenkamp, *Positivism, supra* note 13, at 822; Epstein, *supra* note 60, at 1170; *see also* Katz, *supra* note 13, at 2238 (noting that positive law and economics sees law merely as a set of constraints within which individual citizens maximize).

122 Robert McGee, *Legal Ethics, Business Ethics, and International Trade: Some Neglected Issues*, 10 CARDOZO J. INT'L & COMP. L. 109, 113 ("the criterion for judging whether acts and institutions are just or good is whether they maximize the wealth of society.") (citing RICHARD POSNER, THE ECONOMICS OF JUSTICE, 115 (rev. ed. 1983)); *see also* Hovenkamp, *Positivism, supra* note 13, at 825–26; *see also* Avery Wiener Katz, *Positivism and the Separation of Law and Economics*, 94 MICH. L. REV. 2229, 2248 (1996) (comparing Bentham's nineteenth-century utilitarian that a reasonable comparison of utility across society was possible and would achieve the greatest good for the greatest number of people); *cf.* Jane Rutherford, *The Myth of Due Process*, 72 B.U.L. Rev. 1, 56 (observing that "the most conservative law and economics devotees would reduce all legal questions to one of efficiency.").

123 *See* Epstein, *supra* note 60, at 1172.

Application of law and economics concepts requires acceptance of certain assumptions.[124] Such assumptions include that human wants can be reduced to and accurately measured in economic terms, that human beings are rational actors, and that price theory is accurate and can be applied with specificity to an individual occurrence of human or institutional behavior.[125] Most controversial has been the descriptive claim by some law and economics scholars that the legal system inevitably moves toward an efficient result.[126] Even some prominent law and economics scholars have questioned the validity of that description.[127]

Over time, many of the assumptions of law and economics have come under attack.[128] Some critics have argued that human beings are not rational actors possessing full and

---

124 *See* Hovenkamp, *Antitrust, supra* note 68, at 226–29 (listing basic assumptions of the neoclassical market efficiency model upon which the law and economics school is based).

125 *But see* Hovenkamp, *Positivism, supra* note 13, at 827 (suggesting that the profit-maximization hypothesis is probably not verifiable in any universal sense).

126 *See* Epstein, *supra* note 60, at 1169–70 (describing Posner); Grey, *Langdell's Orthodoxy, supra* note 14, at 51 (noting that Posner finds "efficiency," with all the connotation of approval that term carries in his theory, in the content as well as the methods of Langdellian private law).

127 *See* Epstein, *supra* note 60, at 1170 (arguing that the positive theory of an efficient common law utterly fails to explain why, with transaction costs in decline and information more readily available, judicial regulation should be expected to increase); *see also* John J. Donohue III, *The Law and Economics of Tort Law: The Profound Revolution*, 102 HARV. L. REV. 1047, 1049–50 (1989) (reviewing William M. Landes and RICHARD A. POSNER, THE ECONOMIC STRUCTURE OF TORT LAW (1987)) (comparing Landes and Posner view that tort law is efficient and serves to minimize accident losses and prevention costs with Shavell's more cautious and qualified approach).

128 *See* Katz, *supra* note 13, at 2241 (arguing that methodological reductionism is a model, not a metaphysical truth, and, like all models, aesthetic and pragmatic considerations influence the decision to use it).

complete information.[129] Others have argued that human wants cannot be accurately expressed in economic terms.[130] Still others have expressed concern that those who engage in law and economics fail to test their hypotheses and conclusions with the degree of rigor that economists demand.[131] Finally, an increasing body of literature has argued that institutional interactions are far more complex than the founders of law and economics originally suggested.[132] Despite these

---

129 *See* CASS R. SUNSTEIN, BEHAVIORAL LAW AND ECONOMICS (2000); William J. Barnes, *Revenge on Utilitarianism: Renouncing a Comprehensive Economic Theory of Crime and Punishment*, 74 IND. L.J. 627 (1999) (noting that the "rational actor" assumption makes it difficult for law and economics scholars to produce sound theories in criminal law); Christine Jolls, Cass R. Sunstein & Richard Thaler, *A Behavioral Approach to Law and Economics*, 50 STAN. L. REV. 1471, 1545 (1998) (asserting that rational actors often depart from law and economics' central presumptions of utility maximization, stable preferences, rational expectations, and optimal processing of information as a consequence of bounded rationality, bounded willpower, and bounded self-interest); *see also* Daniel A. Farber, *Playing the Baseline: Civil Rights, Environmental Law, and Statutory Interpretation*, 91 CLMLR 676 (1991) (reviewing CASS R. SUNSTEIN, AFTER THE RIGHTS REVOLUTION: RECONCEIVING THE REGULATORY STATE (1990)); Katz, *supra* note 13, at 2229 (citing scholars who are critical of law and economics' rational choice theory, including Mark Kelman, *Choice and Utility*, 1979 WIS. L. REV. 769 (1979)); Richard H. Pildes & Elizabeth S. Anderson, *Slinging Arrows at Democracy: Social Choice Theory, Value Pluralism, and Democratic Politics*, 90 COLUM. L. REV. 2121 (1990).

130 *See* Hovenkamp, *Positivism*, *supra* note 13, at 836 (arguing that Limiting welfare to wealth maximization amounts to a hopelessly impoverished view of well-being); Nussbaum, *supra* note 13, at 1636 (citing Amartya Sen and describing the difficulty of measuring human welfare).

131 *See* Hovenkamp, *Positivism*, *supra* note 13, at 822v23 (criticizing inadequate hypothesis testing and noting that the danger of dissolving into a kind of "mathematically supported storytelling" is of particular concern in law & economics).

132 Ian Ayres, *Playing Games with the Law*, 42 STAN. L. REV. 1291 (1990) (explaining that game theory challenges law and economics' presumption that market competition is efficient because under certain assumptions markets can fail to promote social welfare); Michael S. Jacobs, *The New*

criticisms, law and economics has had a profound influence on modern legal thought. As described above, modern courts and scholars must now try to manage that economic influence and to make economic insights useful within a judicial setting.[133]

Finally, although less focused on science, one cannot understand twentieth-century legal thought or the current state of legal thought without mention of the critical legal studies (CLS) movement. In addition, understanding the criticisms leveled by the CLS movement is important for understanding the dynamic of what drives us to look for answers in the form of science.

CLS emerged in the 1970s around the same time as law and economics. Unlike the legal realists, CLS scholars did not believe in the complete indeterminacy of language. Rather, CLS argued that even when language and legal rules are crystal clear, law is destined to be inherently contradictory. This contradiction occurs because society is not committed to either a strict rule or a flexible standards approach to the interpretation of law.[134] Vacillation between the two inevitably produces instability on every significant issue, and

---

Sophistication in Antitrust, 79 MINN. L. REV. 1 (1994) (noting that the post-Chicago school builds on the industrial organization approach by challenging that broad generalizations of price theory are inappropriate when small numbers of firms act strategically to exploit market imperfections to the disadvantage of their competitors; Steven C. Salop, *Anticompetitive Overbuying by Power Buyers*, 72 ANTITRUST L.J. 669 (2005) (noting that companies have been known to engage in predatory "overbuying" whereby inputs are purchased solely to deny it to rivals and then discarded); *see also* Epstein, *supra* note 60, at 1174 (a prominent law and economics scholar concluding that the study of legal doctrine and theory has to be enriched with a greater appreciation of institutional arrangements).

133 *See supra* text accompanying notes 68–72 (offering perspectives on current debates in antitrust law).

134 *See* KELMAN, *supra* note 13, at 45.

no resolution is possible.[135] Moreover, the inevitable conflicts cause law to privilege one strain over another for reasons other than objective analysis and logic.

CLS scholars rejected the notion that legal actors could ever objectively study the consequences of alternative legal rules without the distortive effects of the artificial categories that we create and impose on legal questions.[136] Nevertheless, some CLS scholarship reads much like a psychological analysis of human beings, following the social science of the time. Unger, for example, waxes poetic on the notion that the self must seek recognition from others to acquire coherence.[137] Moreover, many CLS scholars advocated exposure and awareness of the bias of legal actors, wherever possible.[138]

---

135 *See id.* at 15 (describing the clash between law's affinity for rules and its attraction to legal standards).

136 *See* KELMAN, *supra* note 13, at 275; *see also* David M. Trubek, *Where the Action is: Critical Legal Studies and Empiricism*, 36 STAN. L. REV. 575, 617–18 (1984) (describing the CLS view that empirical researchers who spend years analyzing the answers to complicated surveys about disputes are like madmen wandering in an asylum that they themselves have constructed).

137 *See* ROBERTO M. UNGER, KNOWLEDGE AND POLITICS 59–60 (1975) ("To deal with the dissolving effect the lack of a finite and coherent system of ends has on its sense of identity, [an individual] must secure the approval of others."); ROBERTO M. UNGER, PASSION: AN ESSAY ON PERSONALITY 97 (1984) ("[people] require not simply an exchange of particular advantages and a recognition of their membership in well-defined communities but also a more radical acceptance of their own selves. They want a sign that there is a place for them in the world, a place where they can undertake certain limited experiments in self-knowledge . . . without risking material and moral disaster.").

138 *See* KELMAN, *supra* note 13, at 275 (noting that abandoning those distortions that we can identify a surely a move towards transformation); David M. Trubek, *Where the Action is: Critical Legal Studies and Empiricism*, 36 STAN. L. REV. 575, 591 (1984) (observing that while critical legal studies scholars seek to show relationships between the world views embedded in modern legal consciousness and domination in capitalist society, they also want to *change* that consciousness and those relationships. Thus, the analysis of legal

Thus, CLS encouraged legal actors to critically examine themselves as a focus of study, despite the inevitable imperfection of the enterprise.

As described above, none of the efforts to make law into a science or to make law more scientific has proven successful. From Langdellian legal science to the progressives' policy science, to the most expansive visions of the law and economics movement, legal theories attempts to emulate science have fallen short.

One could argue that many of the failings of the legal theory movements described above can be attributed, in whole or in part, to issues unrelated to their attempts to emulate science. This is certainly true. Nevertheless, incorporation of science did not solve their problems, although it has remained as a tantalizing strategy that legal theorists return to again and again in different forms.

B. DOCTRINAL EXAMPLES

In addition to the more formal movements, our history abounds with individual moments in which we turn to science to solve law's intractable problems. We are constantly seduced into believing that some new science will provide

consciousness is part of a transformative politics); David S. Caudill, *Disclosing Tilt: A Partial Defense of Critical Legal Studies and a Comparative Introduction to the Philosophy of the Law-Idea*, 72 IOWA L. REV. 287 (1987) (noting that a significant CLS goal is to raise awareness of unexamined, assailable preferences); *see also* G. Edward White, *The Inevitability of Critical Legal Studies*, 36 STAN. L. REV. 649 (1984) (noting that CLS' examination of values extends beyond the individual preferences of legal actors, but also attacks the collective value system of legal culture as a whole); KELMAN, *supra* note 13, at 275 (noting that abandoning those distortions that we can identify surely a move towards transformation).

answers to vexing legal questions, and we are constantly disappointed.

Consider criminal law doctrines concerning the circumstances under which a defendant should be found not guilty by reason of insanity. For more than a century, the American test for criminal insanity flowed from an 1843 British case focused on the question of whether the defendant showed a complete lack of cognitive ability at the time of the crime.[139]

Dissatisfaction with the test swelled in the late 1950s and early 60s, culminating in passage of Section 4.01 of the Model Penal Code.[140] The new test was widely accepted, adopted in almost every federal circuit and in many states as well.[141] It was hailed as a triumph of science. The test was perceived as embodying the latest advances in psychological knowledge and medical thought, ones that would provide authoritative, neutral grounds upon which we could all agree.[142] Science would show us the way through the difficult

139 *See* Julie E. Grachek, *The Insanity Defense in the Twenty-First Century: How Recent United States Supreme Court Case Law Can Improve the System*, 18 In. L.J. 1479, 1483 (2006) (describing history of the modern insanity defense and the M'Naghten test); *see also M'Naghten's Case*, 10 Clark & Fin. 200, 210, 8 Eng. Rep. 718, 722 (1843).

140 Model Penal Code § 4.01(1) (1962) (imposing the standard that the defendant was not responsible if, as a result of mental defect or disease, the defendant lacked substantial capacity to appreciate the criminality of the act or to conform conduct to the requirements of the law).

141 *See* People v. Drew, 22 Cal. 3d 333, 345 (1978)

142 *See, e.g.*, People v. Drew, 22 Cal. 3d 333, 345–47 (1978); United States v. Freeman, 357 F.2d 606, 622 (2nd Cir. N.Y. 1966) (discussing the development of MPC § 4.01); United States v. Chandler, 393 F.2d 920, 926 (4th Cir. Va. 1968) (noting that the new test "substantially meets all of the criticism of the old rules and remedies their presently apparent deficiencies"); Blake v. United States, 407 F.2d 908, 915 (5th Cir. Fla. 1969) (concluding "that [the substantiality type standard of MPC § 4.01] is an appropriate case for adopting a definition of insanity which will serve as a vehicle to enable

question of whether one should be held criminally accountable for one's actions.

The honeymoon was remarkably short lived. By the early 1980s, courts and legislatures, reacting to highly publicized cases in which defendants were found not guilty under the new standard, retreated from the Model Penal Code rule with remarkable speed.[143] California, for example, which had adopted the Model Penal Code test in a case in 1978, returned to the prior test with a ballot initiative four years later.[144]

Our embrace of science and our intense disappointment with the Model Penal Code insanity test reflect the problems of trying to import science for drafting legal rules. The question of whom we should hold criminally responsible for their actions is a question of morality and societal values.[145]

---

the court and jury to give effect to the defense of insanity in terms of what is now known about diseases of the mind.").

143 *See* PAUL APPLEBAUM, ALMOST A REVOLUTION: MENTAL HEALTH LAW AND THE LIMITS OF CHANGE 163–209.

144 *Cf.* People v. Drew, 22 Cal. 3d. 333, 345 (1978) (adopting the Model Penal Code standard) *with* People v. Skinner, 39 Cal. 3d. 765, 768, 776 (1985) (interpreting the 1982 California ballot initiative as intending to return to the M'Naghten standard).

145 *See, e.g.*, State v. Wilson, 700 A.2d 633, 640 (Conn. 1997) ("the proper test must incorporate principles of societal morality"); United States v. Segna, 555 F.2d 226, 233 (9th Cir. Ariz. 1977) (holding that "the district court must . . . instruct on the issue if the record contains evidentiary support for the defendant's theory that, although he realized the offending act was illegal, because of mental disease he possessed a false belief that the act was *morally justified* (emphasis added)"); *see also* Richard E. Redding, *The Brain-Disordered Defendant: Neuroscience and Legal Insanity in the Twenty-First Century*, 56 AM. U. L. REV. 51, 85 (2006) (noting shifts in insanity rules in light of the acquittal of John Hinckley for shooting President Reagan under the Model Penal Codes standard); *cf.* Kaganas, *supra* note 54, at 244–245 (citing the differences among medical definitions of mental illness, legal definitions of insanity and jury verdicts and noting that "[w]hatever the precise test the law may lay down, the sane are divided from the insane according to juries' and judges' ideas about moral responsibility and 'folk

Morality is not easy, and no science can take that burden off the shoulders of the law.

One could argue that the abandonment of the Model Penal Code standard reflected popular overreaction to highly publicized cases rather than a carefully considered rejection of the doctrine based on its inadequacies. Even from this perspective, however, to the extent that science was expected to provide an authoritative and neutral resolution behind which society could rally, it was a dismal failure.

The insanity defense is a particularly good example of law's love affair with science. When struggling to reform the old nineteenth-century test for insanity, courts and scholars not only tried importing science rules to create a test but also tried exporting the problem to scientific experts. For example, two other standards developed in the 1950s and 1960s would have essentially shifted the decision to expert psychiatrists to decide whether the defendant's behavior fit particular psychiatric diagnoses.[146] These were the Durham rule, adopted in a D.C. Circuit case, and the Bonnie Rule, proposed by law professor Richard Bonnie.[147]

---

psychology.' It is 'lay truth' rather than 'law's truth' or 'medical truth' which ultimately prevails.").

146 *See* Michele Cotton, *A Foolish Consistency: Keeping Determinism Out of the Criminal Law*, 15 B.U. Pub. Int. L.J. 1, 7–8 (2005) ("because the Durham rule more closely adhered to psychiatry's deterministic description of human behavior, it unsurprisingly exonerated more defendants than other rules."); Elyn R. Saks, *Competency to Refuse Psychotropic Medication: Three Alternatives to the Law's Cognitive Standard*, 47 U. MIAMI L. REV. 689, 761 n.80 (1993) (discussing "concerns about applying a broad cognitive standard [such as that of the Bonnie test] rather than a volitional standard to cases").

147 *See* Amy D. Gundlack-Evans, *State v. Calin: The Paradox of the Insanity Defense and Guilty but Mentally Ill Statute, Recognizing Impairment Without Affording Treatment*, 51 S. DAKOTA L. REV. 122, 136–37 (2006); *see also* Durham v. United States, 214 F.2d 862 (D.C. Cir. 1954); Richard J. Bonnie, *The Moral*

Attempts to export the insanity defense problem failed as well, burdened by criticism that these approaches would not properly identify those that society wished to hold morally accountable but rather would open the door to excessive acquittals. The Durham rule was reversed by statute and the Bonnie standard was never adopted.[148] In lamenting the failed Durham test, Judge Bazelon, who wrote the Durham opinion, noted that some have described him as "a disappointed lover" after his efforts failed so miserably.[149]

Our legal history is full of such examples in which law, when faced with difficult and unsettling problems, turns to science for a solution, only to find its hopes dashed. For example, indeterminate sentencing and the development of the juvenile court system also were fueled in part by the belief that social scientists could predict and treat.[150] The movement toward indeterminate sentencing came to an abrupt end in the 1970s, among other reasons, because the predictive capacity of social science failed to live up to its

---

Bliss of the Insanity Defense, 69 A.B.A. J. 194, 196–97 (1983); *cf.* Saks, *supra* note 151; Cotton, *supra* note 146.

148 *See* Gundlack-Evans, *supra* note 146, at 137 (noting that "the Bonnie standard was never adopted, and the Durham rule was abrogated by statute"); *see also* United States v. Cohen, 236 U.S. App. D.C. 36 (D.C. Cir. 1984) (noting that D.C. Code § 24-301 "represented a conscious and direct congressional response to [Durham] . . . Congress believed that the Durham test would "result in a flood of acquittals by reason of insanity and fear[ed] that these defendants would be immediately set loose.").

149 Richard Bonnie, *Morality, Equality, and Expertise: Renegotiating the Relationship between Psychiatry and the Criminal Law*, 12 BULL. AM. ACAD. PSYCHIATRY & L. 5–6 (1984); *see* David Bazelon, *Veils, Value and Social Responsibility*, 37 AM. PSYCHOLOGIST 115, 115 (1982). Following that period, lawyers and commentators have been wary of the use of expert testimony by psychologists as a replacement for the statutory measures of elected officials. *See* GARY B. MELTON & JOHN PETRILA, PSYCHOLOGICAL EVALUATIONS FOR THE COURTS: A HANDBOOK FOR MENTAL HEALTH PROFESSIONALS AND LAWYERS 3 (2007).

150 *See* CHRISTOPHER SLOBOGIN & GARY MELTON, PSYCHOLOGICAL EVALUATIONS FOR THE COURTS 251, 418–19.

promise when applied within the justice system.[151] Support for the juvenile justice system has cooled, with the failure of the predictive capacity of social science again playing an important role.[152] Despite these disappointments, there is once again a resurgence of optimism in the predictive capacity of social science indicated by the increasing prominence of the "dangerousness criterion" as justification for confinement, particularly confinement of individuals who have a history of sexual crimes.[153] Again, the legal system asks science to answer whether an individual is imminently dangerous to the community, whether a defendant can be rehabilitated, or whether only incapacitation through incarceration will suffice.

An extreme version of outsourcing legal dilemmas to scientific experts would be allowing a computer system to determine the proper outcome in a case or the proper response to a crime. One need not look to science fiction, however, to find implementation of such a system. The *China Daily* newspaper reported the adoption of a software program in China that recommends criminal sentencing to the judge in an individual case.[154] For example, the program was

---

151 *See* FRANCIS ALLEN, THE DECLINE OF THE REHABILITATIVE IDEAL 8 (1981) (stating that the California sentencing act of 1976 was "representative of a spate of legislative proposals, enacted or advocated throughout the country . . . [attacking] the indeterminate sentence, the parole function, the uses of probation in cases of serious criminality, and even allowances of "good time" credit in the prisons.").

152 *See* SLOBOGIN, *supra* note 150, at 420–21.

153 *See* Christopher Slobogin, *The Civilization of the Criminal Law*, 58 VAND. L. REV. 121(2005) (describing the resurgence of the dangerousness criterion for confinement outside of the traditional incapacitation regimes and arguing in favor of a more forthright adoption of such an approach with individual prevention as the predominant goal of the criminal justice system).

154 Liu Li, *Software Helps Judges Mete Out Sentences*, CHINA DAILY (Sept 7, 2006) available at http://www.chinadaily.com.cn/cndy/2006-09/07/content_683080.htmhttp://www.chinadaily.com.cn/cndy/2006-09/07/content_683080.htm; *see also* Nate Anderson, *China Tests Computer-Aided Sentencing*,

used in the case of a farmer who attacked someone with a knife, injuring his victim slightly in the arm and face. The judge in the case entered the type of crime, the nature of the injury, as well as the fact that the assailant surrendered to police and paid compensation on his own initiative. After three minutes of calculations, the program recommended a 5.4 month prison sentence. The recommendation was not mandatory, however, and the judge imposed a six-month sentence instead. The notion of a computer program dispensing justice is a far cry from the image of law as "the last result of human wisdom acting upon human experience for the benefit of the public."[155]

One might object that it is unfair to invoke examples from the Chinese legal system, whose history and operation is quite distinct from that of the American legal system. The Chinese software program, however, is not that far removed from the Federal Sentencing Guidelines, whose rigid formulas were recently rejected as unconstitutional.[156]

In the context of civil rather than criminal law, the issue of outsourcing legal dilemmas has arisen with the question of what is in the best interests of the child in custody cases. In that arena, courts increasingly lean on experts to decide the underlying issue, an inclination that has proven unsatisfying. As one scholar has noted, "[c]ourts may be only too willing to be relieved of the responsibility of playing

---

ARS TECHNICA (September 14, 2006), http://arstechnica.com/news.ars/post/20060914-7745.htmlhttp://arstechnica.com/news.ars/post/20060914-7745.html.

155 *See* GEORGE BIRKBECK HILL, JOHNSONIAN MISCELLANIES, VOL. 1, 223 (quoting eighteenth-century British author Samuel Johnson); *cf.* BERKOWITZ, *supra* note 86, at ix (quoting Immanuel Kant's description of law as the rational feeling of man's connection with the ideal of justice).

156 *See* United States v. Booker and Unites States v. FanFan, 125 S. Ct. 738 (2005).

guessing games about a child's future if they are persuaded that experts' crystal balls hold the answer."[157] The problem is not just that we are asking scientists to answer legal questions. The problem is also that we are asking scientists to solve our legal quandaries with predictions about human development that they are unable to provide. Outside extreme circumstances such as abuse or neglect, psychology lacks any methodologically sound empirical evidence allowing predictions concerning various custody arrangements.[158]

One of the classic examples of outsourcing legal dilemmas can be found in the Supreme Court's 1954 decision in *Brown v. Board of Education*.[159] The Court held in *Brown* that segregating black school children constituted a violation of the Fourteenth Amendment. The Court found that school segregation "generates a feeling of inferiority as to their status in the community that may affect their hearts and minds in a way unlikely ever to be undone."[160] In support of its finding, the Court cited a series of social science studies in an infamous footnote.[161] As described in more detail in Chapter VI, the Court's use of those studies has been sharply criticized on grounds including that the studies were methodologically unsound and that the data did not support the conclusions drawn from them by the authors of the studies or by the Court.

The Supreme Court's inclination to reach for science in this case, however, is interesting in itself. David Faigman has

157 *See* Lois A. Weithorn, Psychology and Child Custody Determinations 160 (1987).

158 *See id.* at 161.

159 *See* Brown v. Board of Ed., 347 U.S. 483 (1954).

160 *See id.* at 494; *see also* David Faigman, *Normative Constitutional Fact-Finding: Exploring the Empirical Component of Constitutional Interpretation*, 139 U. Pa. L. Rev. 541, 566–73 (1991) (describing *Brown v. Board*).

161 *See* Brown v. Board, 347 U.S. at 494 n.11.

pointed out that the most simple and intriguing explanation of the Court's choice to invoke social science data in *Brown v. Board of Education* rather than simply relying on constitutional principle was the difficulty of choosing a constitutional principle on which to rely.[162] Although scholars have offered many alternative approaches for supporting the Court's decision, they generally do not agree on any single one.[163] Thus, the *Brown* case stands as another example in which the Supreme Court, faced with a contentious social issue and difficult doctrinal issues, wrapped its decision in the cloak of scientific authority. Although no one would argue with the outcome in *Brown*, the scientific wrapping could not solve the Court's problems. Rather, it has created more problems as legal scholars try to grapple with what to do when the result is favored and the scientific basis disfavored, such as trying to create a separate category of so-called interpretive facts that would somehow be distinct from concrete scientific facts.[164] Ronald Dworkin described the category of interpretive facts in the following fashion:

> 'We don't need evidence for the proposition that segregation is an insult to the Black community—we *know* it; we know it the way we know that a cold causes snuffles.' It is not that we don't need to know it nor that there isn't something there to know. There is a fact of the matter, namely that segregation is an insult, but we need no evidence for that fact—we just know it. It's an interpretive fact.[165]

---

162 *See* Faigman, *supra* note 160, at 567–68.

163 *See id.*

164 *See* Ronald Dworkin, *Social Sciences and Constitutional Rights—The Consequences of Uncertainty*, 6 J.L. & EDUC. 3, 5 (1977) (quoting Cahn, *Jurisprudence*, 30 N.Y.U. L. REV. 150, 157–58 (1955)); *see also* Faigman, *supra* note 160, at 560–70 (discussing Dworkin's views of *Brown v. Board*).

165 Dworkin, *supra* note 164, at 5.

Science could not solve our problems in this case, but the importation of science created other problems.

Other examples of law's unsuccessful attempts to reach for science include legal tests imported into law from economic or social science research that are then far too complex to operate in a legal setting. Such rules remain but are noteworthy mostly due to the legal system's inability to apply them with any significant degree of accuracy. Consider the Learned Hand test for negligence liability in tort law. The rule asks that we set negligence at the point where, properly internalized, prevention costs don't exceed accident costs.[166] The ordinary machinery of the legal system has no way to measure that level.[167]

---

166 *See* United States v. Carroll Towing Co., 159 F.2d 169, 173 (2d Cir. N.Y. 1947) (proposing that liability should be established where the burden of adequate precautions is less than the injury multiplied by the probability of the injury's occurrence); *see also* Tsachi Keren-Paz, *An Inquiry into the Merits of Redistribution through Tort Law: Rejecting the Claim of Randomness*, 16 CAN. J.L. & JURIS. 91, 95 (stating that "[t]he Learned Hand formula and its progeny exculpate the defendant from liability when the prevention cost exceeds the expected accident cost."); *cf.* Edward C. Lyons, *Balancing Acts: Intending Good and Foreseeing Harm—The Principle Of Double Effect in the Law of Negligence*, 3 GEO. J.L. & PUB. POL'Y 453, 500 (2005) ("there is no moral indignation in the case in which the cost of prevention would have exceeded the cost of the accident." (quoting Richard A. Posner, *A Theory of Negligence*, 1 J. LEGAL STUDIES 29, 33 (1972)).

167 *See* James M. Anderson, *The Missing Theory of Variable Selection in the Economic Analysis of Tort Law*, 2007 UTAH L. REV. 255, 257 (2007) (noting that there are a nearly infinite number of accident-reducing inputs a court can consider, so decisions over which to consider in the analysis have a central effect on tort analysis); *cf.* Yale Kamisar, *Does (Did) (Should) the Exclusionary Rule Rest on a "Principled Basis" Rather than an "Empirical Proposition"?*, 16 CREIGHTON L. REV. 565, 646 (1983) (observing that "[i]f one is supposed to 'balance' the 'competing interests' before deciding whether to apply the exclusionary rule, how does one do so without measuring imponderables or comparing incommensurables?").

One can also look at rate setting in public utilities regulation, which was described in Stephen Breyer's scholarship prior to joining the bench:

> The possibility of court review has led agencies to keep records demonstrating . . . that [the] decision was rational. . . . Given the multifaceted nature of most problems, the uncertain quality of the information, and the need to consider a broad range of uncertain factors, many technical decisions . . . may reflect only an inspired engineering guess. The engineer may not know precisely where or how the decision emerged—even in his own mind—nor can he necessarily write down a justification for the decision at the time he made it. Thus, records for court review are often made ex post. The agency's lawyers insert into a public record sufficient information to show rational support for each key decision. Cost/benefit analyses are often prepared to support decisions already reached rather than to help determine what future decisions ought to be made.[168]

In short, in both formal legal theory movements and individual moments, law continually turns to science to solve its problems and is frequently dissatisfied. What is important about this pattern is not just our disappointment but our constant return to the well. The repeated behavior reflects both our vision of law and our vision of science in relation to law. We constantly despair of law's inability to resolve legal issues to our satisfaction and view science as a source of rescue from our discontent. It is this particular vision that continually gets us into trouble.

---

168 *See* STEPHEN J. BREYER, REGULATION AND ITS REFORM 117 (1982).

CHAPTER V

The Nature of Law

One cannot determine how to use science appropriately in the domain of law without first considering the nature of law itself. This chapter focuses particularly on the unfolding of case law. This is not to suggest that legislation and administration are any less valid as expressions of the legal process. They do, however, involve specialized considerations beyond the legal behaviors that are the focus of this book.

The art of law involves distilling from prior authorities a common logic that can extend to new circumstances.[169] It is not a scientific expedition but rather a delicate dance of interpretation and adaptation. The enterprise involves identifying relevant groupings that provide comparisons,

169 *Cf.* ANTONIN SCALIA, A MATTER OF INTERPRETATION: FEDERAL COURTS AND THE LAW 8–9 (1997) (comparing the growth of the common law to a Scrabble board in that no rule previously announced can be raised but qualifications can be added. "The first case lays on the board . . . and the game continues").

choosing among the conflicting sets of logic that might emerge, and arguing persuasively for that choice.

In this process, one cannot overestimate the importance of the fact that the issues arising in case law are constantly new. Despite the massive volume of laws and cases, courts are continually faced with new circumstances and new legal issues for two reasons. First, society itself is constantly changing. The domain of interstate commerce, for example, took on an entirely different dimension with the invention of automotive transport.[170] Similarly, the question of what constitutes fair use of one's own copy of a recording must be analyzed differently when anyone with a computer can remix the sounds of the recording.

Consider an example from trademark law. Trademark law protects a trademark holder from others who would use the protected mark in a way that engenders consumer confusion.[171] The arrival of the Internet, however, creates a new level of complexity for the notion of consumer confusion. Suppose I sell cars and operate a Web site advertising my cars. Can I design my Web site so that Internet search engines offer my site as one of the results when someone enters "Toyota" as a search term? Am I violating trademark law even if those who visit my site never see the word "Toyota" and have full knowledge that they are clicking on a competitor rather than Toyota when they click on

---

170 *See* Ollman v. Evans, 750 F.2d 970, 995–96 (D.C. Cir. 1984) (Bork, J., concurring), cert. denied, 471 U.S. 1127 (1985).

Although, in modern American case law, authorities include mainly prior cases and legislation, at times in our history, custom and practice have played a greater role. *See* Lessig, *supra* note 92, at 1403 (noting that prior to 1870, custom held a more central focus in American judicial decision making).

171 *See, e.g.*, Qualitex Co. v. Jacobson Products Co. Inc., 514 U.S. 159 162, 173 (1995) (discussing the Lanham act).

my site?[172] In other words, can trademark law protect Toyota's interests even when, from the consumer's perspective, there is no use of the mark and no confusion? One could not even imagine this question without the invention of the Internet and the advent of search engines.[173]

It is not just technological change but also social change that creates new issues for the courts.[174] Questions concerning fathers' rights and grandparents' rights were unlikely to arise before the decline of the stable family unit in American society in the second half of the twentieth century. This constant march of technological and social change ensures a steady stream of new issues for the courts.

Most important, legal issues are constantly new because the law itself drives both behavior and legal argument into new areas. Judges set boundaries based on the case in front of them. Those wishing to escape the constraints will naturally look for open territory, the interstices among those things that have been decided. In this way, courts are continually driven to evaluate new questions, adapting and interpreting old precedents.

---

172 *See* Margreth Barrett, *Internet Trademark Suits and the Demise of "Trademark Use"*, 39 UC Davis L. Rev. 371, 433–34 (2006) (discussing metatag use); *see also* Brookfield Communications, Inc. v. West Coast Entertainment Corp., 174 F.3d 1036, 1045, 1066–67 (9th Cir. 1999) (finding that the use of a trademark in HTML metatags, invisible to the end user, established the requisite likelihood of consumer confusion); Bihari v. Gross, 119 F. Supp. 2d 309, 312 n.3 (S.D.N.Y. 2000) (explaining the use of metatags to describe the webpage to search engines).

173 For other wonderful examples of questions that could only arise in the modern era, *see* Sonia Katyal, *Semiotic Disobedience*, 84 Wash. U. L. Rev. 489, 495 n.28 (describing artist-activist groups on the web that imitate the operations of a corporation or create fake membership networks).

174 *Cf.* Grey, *Langdell's Orthodoxy*, *supra* note 13, at 39 (noting that Langdell's formalism was not readily adapted to the period of rapid social change in the early years of the twentieth century).

Consider an example from employment law. In the 1980s and 90s, federal courts ruled that employers are strictly liable for sexual harassment that arises from hostile environments created by supervisors.[175] Employers responded by developing internal policies and investigation procedures to find and address bad behavior by supervisors. With this apparatus in place, employers asked the courts to create an affirmative defense to the strict liability. The defense would arise in cases in which employers had created adequate procedures, but the complaining employee had failed to take advantage of what the employer provided. The Supreme Court complied, creating a new defense in response to new forms of corporate behavior.[176] In this example, therefore, both human behavior and legal argument sought available openings in existing case law, and the courts were faced with novel issues.

Law can never be merely the static ordering of what exists. Societal change and human nature guarantee that cases will reach beyond the confines of existing legal doctrine. Novelty alone is not the problem. The problem is that cases will naturally emerge within the spaces created by whatever structure exists, rendering that structure insufficient for resolving the question. This inclination toward the undecided drives the evolution of law and dooms any attempt to capture law within a fixed structure. Thus, law

---

175 *See* Burlington Indus. Inc. v. Ellerth, 524 U.S. 742, 751–61 (1998) (describing the development of direct and vicarious employer liability standards by courts interpreting title VII).

176 *See id.* at 742; *see also* Faragher v. City of Boca Raton, 524 U.S. 775, 807 (allowing an affirmative defense for employers where "the plaintiff employee unreasonably failed to take advantage of any preventive or corrective opportunities provided by the employer or to avoid harm otherwise"); *cf.* State Department of Health Services v. Superior Court of Sacramento County, 31 Cal. 4th 1026, 1049 (2003) (creating a similar defense for employers under California law in the context of damages rather than liability).

cannot fulfill the vision of a great intelligence constantly learning and improving as it builds upon its experience. The pressure of change ensures that law is not a process of perfecting what has gone before but rather a constant struggle to adapt to the new.

This is not to suggest that every case is new. Some legal issues will fall squarely within precedent. Nevertheless, the path of law inevitably moves toward the new and undecided. The art of law involves adapting to those changed circumstances within the framework of what has gone before.

Law is also the engine of its own change, particularly case law. Legal doctrines exist that the average person either may not be aware of or may conveniently avoid thinking about. High-profile cases bring those doctrines to light not by making any changes in the law but simply by illuminating the law that exists. The informational effect of such cases can provoke reform efforts that change the law that existed. This pattern is exemplified in the case of *Kelo v. City of New London*.[177] *Kelo* concerned a city's plan to take possession of private homes through eminent domain for the purpose of transferring the properties to Pfizer Corporation.[178] The transfer was part of a plan to stimulate job growth and increase tax revenues. The Fifth Amendment has been interpreted to forbid states from acquiring property by eminent domain unless the acquisition is for "public use" rather than for the benefit of private individuals.[179] In *Kelo*, the Supreme Court upheld the city's right to take the property by eminent domain, rejecting the landowners' claims that the plan was merely a transfer from one private party to another.[180]

---

177 Kelo v. City of New London, 125 S. Ct. 2655 (2005).

178 *See id.* at 2658–2659.

179 *See id.* at 2672.

180 *See id.* at 2674 (O'Connor, J. dissenting).

Commentators have argued that the *Kelo* decision was no surprise in light of existing Supreme Court doctrines.[181] Nevertheless, the case set off a firestorm of popular protest and law reform efforts. In the two years following the case, twenty-four state legislatures approved state laws imposing greater limits on the state's power of eminent domain than those under the Federal Constitution.[182] Citizens in another eleven states voted on ballot measures to limit the state government's rights of eminent domain, and nine of the ballot measures were approved.[183] By highlighting existing doctrine in a stark manner, the case encouraged the evolution of existing law.

The role of legal academics is also a particularly curious one. As academics, we are never separate observers. It isn't just a question of observational bias, it is a question of observational interference, something that is much more of a problems for law than for science. To expand on a response Judge Easterbrook gave when asked to comment on the process of judging, you get a very different answer if you observe rats running in their mazes than if you ask them about the experience.[184] As legal academics, we are always

181 *See, e.g.*, David Schultz, *Economic Development and Eminent Domain After Kelo: Property Rights and "Public Use" Under State Constitutions*, 11 ALB. L. ENVTL. OUTLOOK 41, 44 (2006) (asserting that the precedents of Berman v. Parker and Hawaii Housing Authority v. Midkiff laid the foundation for the Kelo public use justification for the use of eminent domain for economic development purposes); Jeffery D. Gross and Robert V. Kerrick, *Eminent Domain: Pro: Should Kelo be Condemned? Arizona's Experience with the Public Use Requirement*, 43 AZ ATTORNEY 30, 33 (2006).

182 Margot Roosevelt, *This Land is My Land: How an Eye-Popping Supreme Court Decision Set Off One of This Year's Most Passionate Election Fights*, TIME (Nov. 1, 2006).

183 *See* Roosevelt, *supra* note 182.

184 When asked to comment on a topic related to judicial regulation, Judge Easterbrook replied, "I am, after all, one of the critters under study.

part of the rat pack, and our comments and observations are part of the workings of the system itself.

A. BOUNDED ADAPTATION

As described above, the art of law essentially involves adapting to changed circumstances within the framework of what has gone before. In this process of adaptation, however, is there only one right answer? Will careful legal analysis always point the way to a single result? The Langdellians certainly thought so. Even law and economics can be read to imply that economic analysis, properly applied, can suggest a single most efficient rule choice among the possible options.

The legal realists and progressives, however, did a remarkable job of demonstrating the futility of looking for a single right answer to a particular case.[185] As Holmes argued, outside those cases governed by unambiguously applicable law, plausible deductions can always be constructed on both sides.[186]

How is one to choose? Are the legal realists correct that judicial decision making is essentially unbounded? Are laws and precedents so indeterminate, so capable of a myriad of interpretations that we are left to rely on the unconscious instincts of judges who are merely responding to varying personal prejudices?

It is tempting to succumb to the legal realist vision that law is unconstrained or the even more pessimistic critical legal studies vision of law as inherently unstable and irresolvable.

You should watch the rats run their mazes, not ask them to describe or analyze the experience." *See* Frank H. Easterbrook, *When Does Competition Improve Regulation?*, 52 Emory L.J. 1297, 1297 (2003).

185 *See supra* text accompanying notes 109–12 (discussing the legal realists).

186 *See* Grey, *Langdell's Orthodoxy*, *supra* 13, at 44 (discussing Holmes).

Nevertheless, law is bounded by two significant constraints: the pressure of precedent and the discipline of acceptance.

It is nothing novel to suggest that law is bounded by precedent. Even opinions that appear to deviate from precedent are bathed in language lauding the role of precedent in our legal system.[187] Our commitment to precedent is unquestionable. The more difficult question is whether that commitment is realistic when judges may be consciously or unconsciously pursuing the dictates of their own perspectives and biases. It is the discipline of acceptance, however, that gives strength to our commitment to precedent.[188]

In particular, the final act of the art of law is persuasion and acceptance. In addition to the process of distilling common logic that can extend to new circumstances, the art of law also involves the ability to articulate that common logic in a way that can gain general acceptance. This articulation and confirmation is essential in a system that claims allegiance to precedent, and it reinforces our ability to serve that allegiance.

Different legal actors operate in different acceptance spheres. Lawyers must convince judges. Trial judges convince appellate courts. Appellate judges convince other members of their panels, other members of their circuit, and the

---

187 *See, e.g. infra* text accompanying notes 485–89 (describing how the *Atlantic Thermoplastics* panel ignored the precedent of the *Scripps* case while arguing vigorously that *Scripps* had failed to follow precedent); *see also* Payne v. Tennessee, 501 U.S. 808, 827–28, 111 S.Ct. 2597, 2609, 115 L.Ed.2d 720 (1991) (describing stare decisis as usually the wise policy and the preferred course but not an inexorable command in a decision overruling prior cases holding that Eighth Amendment barred capital sentencing jury from considering "victim impact" evidence).

188 *See* Bix, *supra* note 13, at 898 (describing the view of some legal process scholars that "Reasoned Elaboration," the notion that rules and guidelines involved in judicial decision making are sufficient to create substantial constraint on both process and outcome, will incline courts towards the substantively best outcome).

Supreme Court. The Supreme Court must answer to Congress' ability to initiate constitutional amendments and the president's ability to replace retiring justices with those who hold differing viewpoints. In addition, the entire system is subject to pressure from scholarly and popular commentary.

A variant of this perspective can be found in the views of some legal process scholars who argued that the rules involved in judicial decision making are sufficient to create substantial constraint on both process and outcome. For these scholars, the requirement of "reasoned elaboration" would incline courts toward the substantively best outcome.[189]

The requirement of acceptance mitigates the distortion of personal perspective. Even if judges unconsciously follow their own biases or privilege one strain of conclusions over another, the decisions they reach and the arguments they offer in support must gain the acceptance of others with differing biases.

This perspective softens the bite of some criticisms of legal decision making offered by legal realists, critical legal studies scholars, and those influenced by their scholarship. For example, many scholars have complained that legal analysis is unreliable because it depends on the lens through which one observes the problem. As Katz explained, "one's moral vision of the world necessarily will shape the categories one chooses to describe it."[190] Thus, when Litowitz criticized Ellickson's description of nonlegal rules of behavior in Shasta County, he complained that what Ellickson saw was

---

189 *But see* text accompanying notes 193–95 (noting that the concept I call bounded adaptation does not contemplate inevitable movement toward a best outcome).

190 *See* Katz, *supra* note 13, at 2241.

filtered through distortive models and that only critical models could explain what Ellickson missed.[191] In a similar vein, Unger's seminal Critical Legal Studies piece argues that one cannot rely on reason for objectivity. Rather, reason is infused with subjectivity and the line between reason and desire is artificial.[192]

Despite the power of these observations, the legal system's requirement that one's reason or desire wrapped in reason bounce off of others offers some discipline. It creates an incentive to find that which is more widely acceptable and to readjust when one strays too far into the subjective. One's groupings, whatever they may be, will be subject to the scrutiny of different legal actors with varying experiences and visions, a process that imposes some measure of restraint, although by no means perfect restraint.

The American history of social mobility may also mildly tug against the narrowness of our personal perspectives. The thoughts, "There but for the grace of God go I" or "There with the grace of God will I go someday" may give us a view that supports not only what is in the interests of the position we now occupy but also what is in the interests of the position we could imagine for ourselves.

I have no rose-colored glasses. There will be errors—individual mistakes, collective mistakes, and inabilities to

---

191 *See* Douglas Litowitz, *A Critical Take on Shasta County and the "New Chicago School,"* 15 YALE J.L. & HUMAN. 295, 299 (2003) (arguing that Ellickson missed opportunities to explain "why Shasta County is overwhelmingly white, why it has a brutal history of environmental devastation and genocide against Native Americans, why most of the property owners are men, why it has shocking rates of child poverty and substandard housing, and why it is being overrun with strip malls and low-wage jobs").

192 *See* Unger, *supra* note 137, at 42–43 (discussing the use of reason to analyze desire, and the effect of desire upon reason); KELMAN, *supra* note 13, at 64 (discussing Unger).

reach any position of acceptance at all.[193] Nevertheless, this enterprise of searching for and trying out rational adaptations, unfolding across a span of cases, is at the core of the legal process.

One additional point about the process of acceptance bears mention. Adaptations will be evaluated within the prevailing norms of the society at large or of those within the sphere of acceptance. Thus, there is no assurance that law, as it evolves, will inexorably march toward the better, the more efficient, or the more enlightened. On this point, I agree with the CLS view that there is no uniform evolutionary path upon which societies tend to move and which will incline those societies toward the better.[194] Law may move slightly ahead or lag slightly behind the broader society to the extent that the legal actors who form the more immediate spheres of acceptance are stepping at a different pace from the members of society at large. Nevertheless, law is fundamentally anchored in the past through precedent and limited in its movement by the need for acceptance, defined only by the prevailing moral structures of the relevant society. Thus, although I have much sympathy for the legal process notion that rules and guidelines of discussion and explanation will constrain decision making, I part company on the notion that those constraints are sufficient to lead toward some objective notion of a substantively best outcome.[195]

---

193 Consider, for example, the decades-long struggle over the relationship between Constitutional rights and laws related to abortion.

194 *See* KELMAN, *supra* note 13, at 244 (describing the CLS critique of adaptionist functionalism). This view is in contrast to those law and economics scholars who view the path of law as marching towards greater efficiency in human relations. *See supra* text accompanying notes 119–30.

195 *See* Bix, *supra* note 13, at 89–98 (discussing legal process scholars).

B. IS THERE SOMETHING DIFFERENT ABOUT LAW RELATED TO TECHNOLOGY?

In describing the essential process of law, one might be tempted to ask whether there is something substantially different, however, about law related to technology? Perhaps it is appropriate to defer to science in legal areas related to science, particularly an area such as patent law that involves defining a scientific invention. Laws related to technology, however, are no different from any other areas of law. They require the same tools and proceeds by the same interpretative methods that we employ throughout law as we interpret precedent.

Consider the process of interpreting the meaning of a patent and determining its scope. When delineating the footprint of a patent, one must ask, among other things, what the terms meant to the person who drafted the patent, and whether there are any circumstances in which we would extend that meaning. For example, if a patent holder in the aerospace industry claims a method of calculating something and the patent describes making the calculation at a ground control center, does the patent extend to systems that accomplish the same steps onboard the spacecraft?[196]

In interpreting the scope of the patent language, we could declare that patent drafters must be clear and precise. If they wish to include something, they must describe it directly.[197] Alternatively, we could allow leeway, for example, interpreting language to include shared understandings in the field,

---

196 *See* Hughes Aircraft Co. v. United States, 717 F.2d 1351 (Fed. Cir. 1983).

197 *See, e.g.*, Chiron v. Genentech, 363 F.3d 1247, 1255 (Fed. Cir. 2004) (strictly applying the written description doctrine); Gentry Gallery, Inc. v. Berkline Corp., 134 F.3d 1473 (Fed. Cir. 1998) (same).

even if that information is not directly described in the words of the patent.[198] Reaching even more broadly, we could choose to interpret the language as including something that the drafters did not contemplate, perhaps even unknown at the time of the patent, but that we feel should be within the orbit of the invention. Perhaps the difference is trivial so that the accused device performs the same function in the same way reaching same result as the protected invention.[199] Perhaps there has been an external shock, a fundamental technological change across all industries, such as the advent of digital technology that the drafters of the patent could not have foreseen.[200] We might choose to expand the meaning of the terms to encompass that change if failure to expand would eviscerate the goal of protecting the invention.

Throughout this analysis, patent law is trying to understand terms established at a different time in a different context and apply that understanding to new facts. This enterprise, however, is at the heart of legal reasoning across all areas of

---

198 *See, e.g.*, Amgen Inc. v. Hoechst Marion Roussel, 314 F.3d 1313, 1334 (Fed. Cir. 2003) ("The specification need not explicitly teach those in the art to make and use the invention; the requirement is satisfied if, given what they already know, the specification teaches those in the art enough that they can make and use the invention without 'undue experimentation'"); *cf.* 3 DONALD S. CHISUM, CHISUM ON PATENTS §7.03[2][a] (2003) (noting that in patent law, the hypothetical person skilled in the art is presumed to know all of the prior art in the field).

199 *See* Sanitary Refrigerator, Co. v. Winters, 280 U.S. 30, 42 (1929) (applying the so-called function-way-result test of the doctrine of equivalents).

200 *See Hughes*, 717 F.2d 1351 (Fed. Cir. 1983); *see also* Festo Corp. v. Shoketsu Kinzoku Kogyo Kabushiki Co., 535 U.S. 722, 740 (2002) (a patent holder's decision to narrow claims through amendments at the PTO generally is presumed to be a general disclaimer of territory, but that presumption is rebuttable for things that the patent holder could not have foreseen).

law. It is the essence of interpretation of precedent, whether that precedent is case law, legislation, or the Constitution.[201]

When interpreting a constitutional provision, for example, one might begin by asking what the provision meant to the drafters and whether there are circumstances in which we would extend that meaning.[202] One might decide that the drafters of a constitutional provision or amendment should be clear and precise. If the Constitution grants a power to Congress, for example, that grant must be indicated clearly, or the power is left to the states.[203] One could choose to interpret the language by reference to the social context and the shared understandings of the drafters and their contemporaries.[204] Reaching more broadly, one could

---

201 *Cf.* SmithKline Beecham Corp. v. Apotex Corp., 247 F. Supp. 2d 1011 (N.D.Ill.2003) (Posner, J. sitting by designation) (noting that the Federal Circuit deems statutory interpretation a useful analogy to claim construction and citing Markman v. Westview Instruments, Inc., 52 F.3d 967, 987 (Fed.Cir.1995), *aff'd*, 517 U.S. 370, 116 S.Ct. 1384, 134 L.Ed.2d 577 (1996)); Margaret Jane Radin, *The Linguistic Turn In Patent Law* 5 (manuscript on file with author) (comparing patents to statutes and contracts and arguing that the relationship of patents to the objects they cover is not unique).
See Hughes, 717 F.2d 1351 (Fed. Cir. 1983).

202 *See* Lessig, *supra* note 92, at 1373 (explaining that the two basic steps in constitutional interpretation are to locate a meaning in an original context and then to ask how that meaning is to be carried to a current context).

203 *See* Martin v. Hunter's Lessee, 14 U.S. 304, 326 (holding that "[t]he government, then, of the United States, can claim no powers which are not granted to it by the constitution, and the powers actually granted, must be such as are expressly given, or given by necessary implication"); *cf.*, Deepsouth Packing Corp. v. Laitram Corp., 406 U.S. 518 (1972) (holding in a legislative interpretation case that if Congress wants § 271 of the patent act to apply outside US territory, it must say so explicitly).

204 *See* Powell v. McCormack, 395 U.S. 486, 522–48, 89 S.Ct. 1944, 1964–77, 23 L.Ed.2d 491 (1969) (examining English precedent, Constitutional Convention debates, and post-Convention ratification debates in interpreting the Qualification Clauses of Art. I in striking down a House resolution prohibiting elected representative from taking his seat).

choose to expand what would have been part of the shared understandings at the time of the drafters in light of changed circumstances in society and to give effect to the provision. Lessig offers a simple example of the third approach: Article I of the Constitution, which speaks of the army and navy, might reasonably be interpreted to include the air force, considering that the army and navy constituted the full complement of armed forces at the time of the Constitution whereas our nation's armed forces now include an Air Force given the advent of military flight.[205] As Judge Bork explained:

> Judges given stewardship of a constitutional provision-such as the first amendment-whose core is known but whose outer reach and contours are ill-defined, face the never-ending task of discerning the meaning of the provision . . . it is the task of the judge in this generation to discern how the framers' values, defined in the context of the world they knew, apply to the world we know. The world changes in which unchanging values find their application. . . . The first amendment's guarantee of freedom of the press was written by men who had not the remotest idea of modern forms of communication. But that does not make it wrong for a judge to find the values of the first amendment relevant to radio and television broadcasting. . . . Perhaps the framers did not envision libel actions as a major threat to that freedom. I may grant that, for the sake of the point to be made. But if, over time, the libel action becomes a threat to the central meaning of the first amendment, why should not judges adapt their doctrines?[206]

---

205 *See* U.S. CONST. art. I.; Lessig, *supra* note 92, at 1376–77.

206 *See* Ollman v. Evans, 750 F.2d 970, 995–96 (D.C. Cir. 1984) (Bork, J., concurring), *cert. denied*, 471 U.S. 1127 (1985).

The question of whether, how far, and under what circumstances we might expand application of a constitutional provision is a question that must be answered by legal theory and doctrine. No linguistics expert or other social scientist can answer the question for us.[207]

Patent interpretation is like constitutional interpretation at hyper speed. With a patent, we are trying to interpret a document, and the extent of rights granted with that document, in the context of rapidly changing meaning and knowledge. In this enterprise science can offer only limited assistance. Science, whether biochemistry or linguistics, can help identify the ways in which things are different or the same, but it cannot tell us the legal implications of those similarities or distinctions.

Thus, even in patent law, where the logic for using to science is at its strongest, the enterprise remains the same process of legal analysis and adaptation that we engage in throughout the law.

C. THE MISMATCH OF LAW AND SCIENCE

As described above, law is constantly driven to adapt to changing circumstances within existing frameworks as tested and refined through various spheres of acceptance. Science rules are particularly ill suited to this process of adaptation.[208]

---

207 One can analogize to interpretation of a contract. A linguist can offer us varying interpretations of the words, but the questions such as what we understand the context of the agreement to be, and how much that matters, and when we will look outside the contract can only be answered by legal analysis.

208 *Cf.* Roscoe Pound, *Mechanical Jurisprudence*, 8 Colum. L. Rev. 605, 606 (1908) (arguing that "[p]erfection of scientific system and exposition tends to cut off individual initiative in the future, to stifle independent consideration of new problems and of new phases of old problems, and to impose the ideas of one generation upon another").

If legal actors lack sufficient information about a rule to both adapt it and to challenge those adaptations, the use of that rule will interfere with the unfolding of the legal process. Thus, science rules and terms, which embody assumptions and shared understandings beyond the legal realm, hinder this process. Most important, as described above, reaching for science can create the illusion of reasonable resolution without addressing the true problems at stake. The lack of analysis gives us insufficient information upon which to build and develop legal theories, leaving us to cling to rigid lines of demarcation instead.

The mismatch of law and science is particularly problematic in the modern legal system. Developments in philosophy of science over more than the last fifty years have radically altered our understanding of the nature of science, the difference between science and pseudo-science, and the limitations of any scientific endeavor. Law, however, maintains a pure and idealized vision of science, one that is far removed from any contemporary understanding within the scientific field itself. Thus, the problem is not only that science cannot do for law what we think it can, the problem is also that science is not even what we think it is. The following chapter explores the development of science as a separate intellectual discipline to illustrate the significant gaps between law's vision of science and the reality of science.

CHAPTER VI

What is Science?

> *"Science is a phenomenon that has developed through the ages-dragging itself apart from religion, philosophy, superstition, and other bodies of human opinion and belief."*
>
> Michael Ruse[209]

One cannot explore the role of science in anything without first asking, "What is science?" The question is more difficult than it might appear. The notion of what constitutes science has perplexed philosophers across hundreds of years of human history—often in the context of trying to identify what is *not* science. In particular, the last half-century has witnessed nothing short of a revolution in thinking about what constitutes science. The upheaval has left philosophers and scientists without agreement on a coherent definition of science.

To illustrate the problems, let me offer two stories. In the first, a man is walking down a suburban street rubbing two sticks together. A passerby asks the man what he is doing, and the man replies that he is keeping elephants away. The passerby scoffs, "How in the world can rubbing sticks

---

209 Michael Ruse, *Creation-Science Is Not Science*, 7 SCIENCE, TECHNOLOGY, & HUMAN VALUES no. 40, 72, 72 (Summer 1982).

together keep elephants away?" The man replies: "Do you see any elephants?"

In the second story, imagine that a scientist living long before the invention of the microscope theorizes the existence of bugs smaller than lice that live in or on our bodies and make us sick.[210] He designates these bugs "crobes" and develops health recommendations based on their existence, including that healthy people should avoid contact with the sick and that anyone coming in contact with the sick should wash their hands and their clothing. The recommendations lead to a reduction in the spread of disease. In looking at the two stories, how do we develop criteria to decide what constitutes science and what does not?

Although the question of what constitutes science is devilishly complex, the inquiry for our purposes is somewhat simpler. The ultimate question is not so much what is science but rather, what does law *think* science is and what are the gaps between that vision and our modern understanding of science.

Law's definition of science is fairly uncluttered. It is nicely reflected in a contemporary court's definition of science as "the process by which knowledge is systematized or classified through the use of observation, experimentation, or reasoning."[211] As one author explained very simply in a book concerning what lawyers need to know about science, "Science is the best way to understand the way the world works. It has had enormous success in explaining physical, chemical and biological processes . . . though there remain great areas of ignorance."[212]

---

210 This story is adapted from Stephen Toulmin, *Do Sub-Microscopic Entities Exist?, in* KLEMKE, *supra* note 49, at 358, 363–365.

211 ITT Research Inst. v. U.S., 9 Cl. Ct. 13, 20 (1985).

212 *See* Lewis Wolpert, *What Lawyers Need to Know About Science, in* REECE, *supra* note 53, at 289.

Thus, law's definition of science begins with the notion that society possesses knowledge, that is, things that are both knowable and true. Science then has the capacity to add to that knowledge and to organize it in a way that is manageable and can lead to future insights. Its methods of organization are grounded in objectivity, which generate confidence in the reliability of its results.

Implicit in the definition is the notion that science is cumulative and progressive. In other words, the body of knowledge that science offers continues to build on the knowledge that comes before leading us to an increased understanding of the world around us. It calls to mind an image of scientists tinkering with old insights and adding new revelations. In the words of one author, "[s]cience is progressive . . . approach[ing] closer and closer to understanding the nature of the world."[213] As Sarton explained in describing scientists, "[w]e do our best to approach the truth by successive approximations; we do not claim to have the truth, but we are reaching for it, and coming gradually closer to it. We do not start with the whole truth, but we obtain more and more of it."[214]

Also implicit in law's definition of science is a veneration of things scientific and a separation from those things that are not science. Science is something of value, in which we can have confidence. As one author has noted "[a]lthough [science's] conclusions may be speculative, provisional, and subject to modification, science is ordinarily seen as set apart from all other social activities by virtue of its institutionalized

213 *See* Wolpert, *supra* note 212, at 289; *see also* Jon Frauley, *Towards an Archaeological-Realist Foucauldian Analytics of Government*, 47 BRITISH J. CRIM. 617, 617 (July 2007) (describing tenets of critical realism including that there is an objective truth and science undergoes continual revision toward a better, although imperfect, understanding of it).

214 *See* SARTON, *supra* note 51, at 417.

procedures for overcoming particularity and context dependence and its capacity for generating claims of universal validity."[215] In other words, science and scientific methods help us get to information that is reliable, sustainable and true in some absolute sense.

This definition of science probably feels comfortable and familiar to a legal audience, but it varies significantly from the view of science held within the world of science today. To illuminate these differences, this chapter explores the evolution of Western civilization's views on what is science.

The chapter is not intended to provide a comprehensive history of science or a thorough understanding of the modern field known as the philosophy of science. Both of these areas are admirably covered by other authors.[216] Rather, the chapter is intended to highlight key moments in which science emerges and separates from other types of intellectual inquiry. In particular, the chapter focuses on three periods of history that are critical to the development of the law/science relationship: ancient Greece, the Scientific Revolution in Europe, and twentieth-century reevaluations of the meaning of science. In highly simplified form, what we think of as science today begins its history deeply entwined with philosophy and theology. During the Scientific Revolution, science begins to separate from other types of intellectual endeavor, although the lines of demarcation are

---

215 JASANOFF, *supra* note 52, at 7.

216 For thorough and fascinating views of the history of science, *see* the two-volume set, SARTON, A HISTORY OF SCIENCE (1952) as well as A. WOLF, THE HISTORY OF SCIENCE TECHNOLOGY, AND PHILOSOPHY IN THE 16TH & 17TH CENTURIES (1935). For comprehensive sets of readings that introduce the field of philosophy of science, *see* MARTIN CURD & J.A. COVER, PHILOSOPHY OF SCIENCE: THE CENTRAL ISSUES (1998); KLEMKE, *supra* note 49; *see also* ALEX ROSENBERG, PHILOSOPHY OF SCIENCE: A CONTEMPORARY INTRODUCTION (2d ed., 2005).

never solid. In the mid-twentieth century, philosophers challenge the notion that science is so neatly discreet, although they are unable to settle on a coherent definition. An uneasy truce develops in which science can be defined as a cluster of concepts, albeit ones that do not work individually or even as a whole. For our purposes, the important point is the following: Those things that make science what it is, are a far cry from law's vision of science. Distortions in law's understanding of the nature of science magnify the problems created when law reaches for science to solve its problems.

A. SCIENCE IN ANCIENT HISTORY

> *A physicist, a biologist and a mathematician walk into a bar. Bartender says, "Any of you believe in God?" Which of the three is most likely to say yes?*
> *Answer: The mathematician. . . . Most mathematicians believe in heaven. Not a heaven with angels, but one populated by the abstract objects they devote themselves to studying. . . their mathematical heaven resembles the realm of the Good and the True described in Plato's "Republic."*[217]

Although stirrings of science undoubtedly exist throughout human history, most historians trace the development of what we think of as science to the time of ancient Greece.[218] This is the period, for example, of the development of

217 Jim Holt, *Proof: A Mathematician Tries to Refute the Arguments for the Existence of God*, N.Y. TIMES, Jan. 13, 2008, Book Review at 18.

218 This includes both the Classical Period from 490–336 BC and the Hellenistic Period from 336–146 BC. JOHN FREELY, THE CYCLADES: DISCOVERING THE GREEK ISLANDS OF THE AEGEAN 241 (2006). For extensive explorations of the development of science in ancient Greece, *see* ANTHONY ALIOTO, A HISTORY OF WESTERN SCIENCE (1987); DAVID C. LINDBERG, THE BEGINNINGS OF WESTERN SCIENCE (1991); G.E.R. LLOYD, EARLY GREEK SCIENCE: THALES

Euclidean geometry as a systematic exploration of the relationships of items in space.[219] In various disciplines, the Greeks worked to combine theorems into a single system in which one could reach individual conclusions by reasoning from a series of first-order principles.[220] In other words, rather than simply observing natural phenomena, Greek philosophers searched for theories to describe the functioning of particular systems as a whole and the interrelationships of the various parts. Greek philosophers coined the word "cosmos," a term that implies a well-ordered and harmonious system, to describe the universe.[221]

Some philosophers in this period framed their inquiries in terms of looking for the overall purpose of the elements of nature. The natural world was not a collection of discrete elements but an ordered hierarchy in which each individual piece was related to the fulfillment of some purposed beyond itself.[222] For some, the entire cosmic scheme was a hierarchy of purposes culminating in the supreme "good" toward which creation moves.[223]

TO ARISTOTLE (1970); G.E.R. LLOYD, GREEK SCIENCE AFTER ARISTOTLE 91973); OLAF PEDERSEN, EARLY PHYSICS AND ASTRONOMY (1974).

219 *See* W.T. JONES, A HISTORY OF WESTERN PHILOSOPHY: THE CLASSICAL MIND, 20 (2d ed. 1970) (noting that while it is not known who first succeeded in systematizing geometry into one axiomatic system, the oldest extant text that does it is Euclid's *Elements*, written about 300 BC). Jones explains that Euclid's work was so impressive that most Western philosophers have regarded it as the paradigm of human reasoning. *See id.*

220 *See* JONES, *supra* note 219, at 20.

221 *See* 2 ROUTLEDGE ENCYCLOPEDIA OF PHILOSOPHY 677–678 (Edward Craig ed. 1998); SARTON, *supra* note 51, at 287. Specifically, Thales is said by later writers to have been the first to use this word. It is significant that the word is never used to describe the universe as a well-ordered whole in Homer, who uses the notion only to describe anything deemed beautiful because orderly, following a notion similar to the roots of our word "cosmetics."

222 *See* JONES, *supra* note 219, at 221 (describing Aristotelian logic).

223 *See* WOLF, *supra* note 216, at 5 (describing Platonic thought and its later influence on the European thought in the medieval period).

As one scholar has explained, early thinking in this period combined a theological notion of a unifying force in the universe with a secular directive to seek this principle not in divine doings but in natural events and processes.[224] What is natural is good, and a full understanding of any natural thing would include understanding its interrelation to the purposes and ordering principles of everything.[225]

In the search for first-order principles, Greek thinkers began to engage in abstraction of observed phenomena.[226] This form of thinking in abstractions allowed those who studied physics and the nature of the universe to entertain theories that collided with ordinary perception.[227] It fostered significant advances not just in scientific but also in philosophical thought.

Despite the remarkable advances in mathematics, physics, astronomy, and other scientific fields, views of science in Ancient Greece vary greatly from modern views of science. Although approaches vary among different schools of Greek thought, some of the strains are strikingly different from the way we view science today. These differences include images of the types of issues that are of greatest value to society, the types of knowledge humans can obtain with any degree of reliability, and the best methods of obtaining that knowledge.

---

224 *See* JONES, *supra* note 219, at 9 (discussing the work of the pre-Socratic Greek philosopher Thales).

225 *See* KLEMKE, *supra* note 49, at 483 (describing Ancient Greek views on science and explaining that there was no differentiation between what we consider scientific knowledge and knowledge of values and what is good.).

226 *See* JONES, *supra* note 224, at 337 (noting that higher mathematics for the Greeks was an instrument directed less to the conquest of the physical environment than to the intellectual construction of an abstract world).

227 *See* JONES, *supra* note 219, at 21 (discussing ancient Greek physicists and cosmologists whose conclusions conflicted with perceptions in contrast to the mathematicians whose conclusions generally agreed with sense experience);

The themes described below represent only threads of Ancient Greek thought about science, and there are certainly many others. Nevertheless, they demonstrate Western society's early struggles to conceptualize the role that science should play in relationship to issues of justice and morality, things that we associate with law in the modern world, and they provide some interesting contrasts to our modern viewpoints.

For understanding contrasts between ancient and modern views of science, one could begin with the Greek philosopher Socrates and his elevation of what we would think of as philosophic inquiry over scientific inquiry. Socrates criticized those who studied the movements of the planets and the intricacies of weather patterns, arguing that the workings of the divine universe are unknowable to man.[228] "Do those who pry into heavenly phenomena imagine that once they have discovered the laws by which these are produced, they will create at their will, winds, waters, seasons, and such things to their need?"[229]

In support of the notion that the laws of nature are unknowable, Socrates pointed out that those who engage in the study of natural phenomena cannot agree and appear "as madmen" to each other.[230] If they appear as madmen to each other, perhaps we should recognize their entire enterprise as lunacy.

More than just a waste of time, however, Socrates believed that those who study nature and the universe are neglecting

228 *See* XENOPHON, MEMORABILIA 11 (E.C. Marchant trans., Harvard University Press 1997) (describing the Socratic belief that human beings should not waste time contemplating the heavens).

229 *See* SARTON, *supra* note 216, at 20.

230 *See* PAUL A. VANDER WAERDT, THE SOCRATIC MOVEMENT 80 (Cornell University Press 1994).

their duty to contemplate issues of true importance to society.[231] Courage and cowardice, justice and injustice are the questions that should occupy our minds not inquiries about the laws of the universe.[232]

The Socratic view of science, of course, is a distinctly different view from the one generally held in the modern world. Across the millennia, we have gained confidence in our ability to understand the laws of nature and developed the optimism to believe we can change water and wind, if not the weather. Science seems knowable, while contemplation of the nature of justice seems more like a topic of idle speculation, full of unanswerable questions to which no resolution is possible. It is in that realm we are bound to appear as madmen to each other.[233] Moreover, Socrates' notion of what is more valuable to society and what is less valuable turns the modern view on its head. In the modern hierarchy, it is the scientists we revere the most and whose work we believe is of greatest value to society.

In addition to Socratic views of science, the Platonic thread of ancient Greek thought provides its own contrast to modern views, particularly on the question of the best method of obtaining reliable information. Plato argued that reliable information cannot be obtained from observing objects in the world around us. In Plato's view, the world we can study with our senses is subject to corruption and death.[234] It is only ideas, the abstractions of what we can

---

231 *See* SARTON, *supra* note 216, at 20.

232 *See id.* at 20, 262.

233 *Cf. supra* text accompanying notes 103–109 (describing the legal realist viewpoint that laws and precedents are indeterminate and capable of a myriad of interpretations).

234 *See* SARTON, *supra* note 216, at 402.

identify with our senses, that are real and permanent and that lend themselves to classification and hierarchy.[235]

As Plato explained, the horse that we can see with our own eyes is only an appearance, like a shadow in a cave.[236] The idea of a horse, however, is constant and eternal, the archetype of all horses born and unborn.[237] The idea allows us to think about and classify objects in their full nature, rather than being limited by one evanescent appearance.[238]

The notion of trying to gain a comprehensive understanding by studying all variations of a category is not unfamiliar to modern science. More striking, however, is the difference in the recommended methods for reaching that more comprehensive understanding. Modern scientists, and those who would emulate science, value the precise analysis and categorization of objects and phenomena that can be observed through our senses and instruments. The same is true for those who labor to make modern law more scientific. The focus is on empirical analysis of things that can be verified. In the modern world of empirical legal analysis, justice is to be found not in the abstraction of the reality around us but in the precise measurement and quantification of those things that are concrete or that can be concretized. For better or worse, it is the opposite of Plato's vision.

---

235 *See* ALIOTO, *supra* note 218, at 43; SARTON, *supra* note 216, at 402–03; *see also* KLEMKE, *supra* note 49, at 483 (noting that for Plato, what is "most real" is the most abstract and the least accessible to ordinary experience).

236 *See* ALIOTO, *supra* note 218, at 43; SARTON, *supra* note 216, at 402.

237 *See id.*

238 *See id*; *see also* ALIOTO, *supra* note 218, at 43 (describing Plato's famous analogy from THE REPUBLIC in which Plato argued that those who do not separate the universal forms from their material instances are like prisoners in a cave, with their backs to the fire, looking forward at a cave wall, and seeing only shadows of the real things behind them).

One notion of Plato's, however, seems to endure in the modern vision of science, although perhaps not in the form of any direct homage to Plato. Plato argued that those who see the idea of virtue will themselves be virtuous, for no one who has attained such knowledge could easily do wrong.[239] The same notion runs through law's love affair with science. Scientific knowledge is most highly valued, and those who have scientific knowledge are surrounded with an aura of wisdom by virtue of their engagement in what we see as a purer type of pursuit. In more rational or palatable form, we reassure ourselves that those who have learned how to engage in/obtained knowledge of objective and reliable scientific methodology will have the clarity and objectivity to resolve our legal dilemmas as well. Our faith, however, relies on the assumption that the scientific wisdom is indeed as pure as we imagine and that the scientific pursuit translates well into the legal realm. Only then could wisdom gained through the pursuit of science translate into a generalized form of wisdom that could lead scientists to a more just resolution of our legal dilemmas.

Despite the Socratic and Platonic devaluation of the study of natural phenomena in comparison with philosophic inquires, other pre- and post-Socratic movements provide a warmer embrace for the emerging fields of what we now think of as scientific inquiry. Following on the heels of Plato, Aristotelian writings reject the Platonic veneration of ideas and wholeheartedly embrace the precise study of natural

239 *See* SARTON, *supra* note 216, at 403. Although Plato may have been referring only to a phenomenon in which knowing about *virtue* affects the human character, there is a subtle implication that those who obtain knowledge of the most valuable kind are themselves essentially good. *See id; see also* ALIOTO, *supra* note 218, at 42 (explaining that for Plato, virtue was knowledge and that knowledge provides an awareness of how to act virtuously).

phenomena. Creating encyclopedic treatises on physics, astronomy, zoology, psychology, and more, Aristotle studied the natural world, not as an end in itself, but as a way to understand the causes responsible for natural phenomena and to see how such phenomena condition and produce each other.[240] Aristotle's notion of causation included images of the divine, but such imagery bears little resemblance to that of the modern Christina deity.[241] Aristotle's "Prime Mover", for example, is a living deity, totally absorbed in self-contemplation, who does not know of the existence of human beings and does not intervene on their behalf.[242] The Prime Mover influences celestial movement not by contacting or intending to effect celestial bodies but simply by existing as an object of desire. Celestial spheres try to imitate the Prime Mover's perfection by assuming uniform, circular motions.[243] Thus, although Aristotle resurrected science as essential to intelligent inquiry, scientific observation was intertwined with contemplation of the divine.

Aristotle's notion of science included topics related to justice and political theory, and he adopted the same observational approach in those arenas. With the help of his students, for example, he compiled accounts of hundreds of *politeiai*, arrangements specifiying the use of power in a

---

240 *See* PEDERSEN, *supra* note 218, at 31; LINDBERG, *supra* note 218, at 64. For a discussion of Aristotle's notion of causes, *see* LLOYD, EARLY GREEK SCIENCE: THALES TO ARISTOTLE, *supra* note 218, at 105-107.

241 *See* LLOYD, EARLY GREEK SCIENCE: THALES TO ARISTOTLE, *supra* note 218, at 107 (explaining that Aristotle postulates no divine mind controlling natural changes from the outside); *see also* LINDBERG, *supra* note 218, at 220 (noting that Aristotle's Prime Mover is "a far cry from the Christian God, who knows when the sparrow falls and numbers the very hairs on our head.").

242 *See* LINDBERG, *supra* note 218, at 62, 220.

243 *See id.* at 62.

particular state.[244] Unlike Plato, who started by contemplating what the Good and the Just *ought* to be, Aristotle surveyed actual political arrangements across hundreds of communities.

In short, the period of ancient Greece, from the Classical Period until the Roman domination, marks the development of the types of systematic exploration and organization of knowledge about the natural world that we think of as science today. It also marks the beginning of society's struggle to think about scientific knowledge in relationship to issues such as justice and morality that we often associate with law today. Those early stirrings about what knowledge is important, what knowledge is attainable, and how one should go about obtaining such knowledge vary tremendously from their modern counterparts. Most important, under the dominant strain of Greek philosophical thought at the end of this period, science was strongly intertwined with understanding the divine through the workings of the natural world.

B. THE SEPARATION OF SCIENCE

Ancient Greece marked the beginnings of studying various types of natural phenomena as systematic and organized bodies of thought. Nevertheless, these bodies of thought, which we think of as science today, did not separate from other types of thought until the Scientific Revolution in Europe in the 1500s and 1600s.

---

244 *See* ARISTOTLE, THE POLITICS 55-86 (Carnes Lord Trans. with intro, notes, and glossary 1984); *see also* MICHAEL DAVIS, THE POLITICS OF PHILOSOPHY: A COMMENTARY ON ARISTOTLE'S *POLITICS* (1996) 33-45 (describing Aristotle's second book of the POLITICS which contains the survey of *politeiai*);

At the opening of this period in Europe, the term "philosophy" was still used to describe both things that we would consider philosophy and things that we would consider science.[245] Not only were science and philosophy intertwined, all intellectual inquiry was considered subordinate to the theology of the Christian Church.

The European masses at the time were living in brutal circumstances.[246] Against the backdrop of their wretched conditions, the Church counseled the faithful to focus on the life hereafter. As one scholar explains:

> The Earth was of little interest in comparison to Heaven. The present life was at best a preparation for the life hereafter. And the Church claimed absolute authority for truths revealed by the light of grace, in comparison with which the light of reason was of no consequence.[247]

Thus, in the hierarchy of intellectual endeavors of the time, the most important and revered knowledge was theological. Although human beings could access such knowledge, the method of access was limited to revelation by the grace of God and through the Church.

In contrast, rational knowledge, obtained through the human mind's ability to perceive objects or to reason, occupied a far more lowly status.[248] In addition, although the Church acknowledged a separate realm of thought outside of the theological, Church authority extended to that realm as well.[249] In particular, the Church set up Aristotelian thought as authoritative on matters both philosophical and

---

245 *See* WOLF, *supra* note 216, at 1.

246 *See id.* at 634.

247 *See id.* at 2.

248 *See id.* at 629.

249 *See id.*

scientific that did not conflict with the Church theology using its own particular interpretation of Aristotle.

As Europe emerged from the mediaeval period, however, science began the slow process of pulling away, first from the hand of the Church and then from philosophy's embrace. In the process, science established an identity for itself. This identity was centered on developing theories from observable facts and experimentation and distinguished from both the theological revelations of the Church and the more speculative and contemplative inquiries of philosophy.[250] By this separation, science divorced itself from many of the issues related to justice and morality that flow into modern conceptions of legal standards.

In most cases, the men of the scientific revolution were deeply religious and loyal sons of the church.[251] They operated under the assumption that the study of nature could only reveal the majesty of the divine. Observation, however, quickly outpaced revelation in this period, and scientific insights threatened to conflict with Church dogma.

The conflict emerged when Copernicus developed his astounding theory that the earth and the planets revolve around the sun.[252] Copernicus was not an anti-Church

---

250 *See, e.g.*, RENE DESCARTES, DISCOURSE ON METHOD AND THE MEDITATIONS 21 (John Veitch trans. 1989). For a general discussion of intellectual thought during this period, *see* STEPHEN GAUKROGER, DESCARTES: AN INTELLECTUAL BIOGRAPHY 116 (1995).

251 *See* WOLF, *supra* note 216, at 2–3.

252 *See, e.g.*, WOLF, *supra* note 216, at 5–6 (noting that the first great scientific move of the period occurred around the middle of the 16th century with publication of Copernicus' theory of heliocentricity); MARCIA SWEET STAYER, NEWTON'S DREAM 5 (1988) (stating that "[n]early everyone takes Copernicus as the beginning of the scientific revolution"); JACK REPCHECK, COPERNICUS' SECRET: HOW THE SCIENTIFIC REVOLUTION BEGAN 10 (2007) (stating that "the beginning of the scientific revolution would have been different and surely would have been delayed if the manuscript for *On the*

reactionary, and he did not set out to contradict the Church.[253] He was trying to solve the problem of the seemingly erratic movement of the planets and the increasingly unreliable calendar.[254] Nevertheless, Copernicus recognized the explosive potential of his theories and, for much of his life, was reluctant to widely publish his insights.[255]

Why was the notion that the earth moves around the sun such an explosive concept? To begin with, it contradicts visual perception. The earth around us appears still while the sun clearly seems to march across the sky.[256] Most important, heliocentricity cast doubt on central Christian doctrines. If God created man in his image and at the center of the universe, the earth must be at the center as well.[257] In fact, the notion of the earth moving at all conflicts with scripture. As Martin Luther noted in criticizing Copernicus, "the fool

---

Revolutions had not been published when it was"). The Copernican revolution is followed over the next two centuries by equally astounding advancements in physics, chemistry, and to some extent biology, as well as other advancements in astronomy. *See* WOLF, *supra* note 216, at 5–6.

253 *See* RICHARD TARNAS, THE PASSION OF THE WESTERN MIND: UNDERSTANDING THE IDEAS THAT HAVE SHAPED OUR WORLD VIEW 251 (1991) (noting that Copernicus was a canon in good standing of Catholic cathedral and an esteemed consultant to the church in Rome).

254 *See id.* at 248–59.

255 *See id.* at 251 (citing Copernicus' own explanation in his preface to *De Revolutionibus*); *see also* NICHOLAS COPERNICUS, PREFACE AND DEDICATION TO POPE PAUL III, ON THE REVOLUTIONS OF HEAVENLY SPHERES (1543), *translated in* STEPHEN HAWKING, ON THE SHOULDERS OF GIANTS 2–6 (Running Press 2002) (stating "I was in great difficulty as to whether I should bring to light my commentaries written to demonstrate the Earth's movements").

256 *See* Philip G. Frank, *The Variety of Reasons for the Acceptance of Scientific Theories, in* KLEMKE, *supra* note 49, at 468–69 (noting that even Francis Bacon rejected the Copernican system because it was not compatible with common sense).

257 *See* TARNAS, *supra* note 253, at 253.

will overturn the whole science of astronomy. But as the Holy Scripture states, Joshua bade the sun stand still and not the earth."[258]

As revealed in the Psalms, "the world is firmly established, it cannot be moved."[259] By conflicting with the light of revelation revealed in scripture, emerging science had the potential to challenge the tightly woven authority of the Catholic Church. The scientific challenge came at a time when Protestant reformers were mounting an attack on the authority of the Catholic Church, an attack wrapped in criticism of the Church's failure to follow literal scripture.[260]

Over the next hundred years, some of the greatest names in scientific history, including Galileo, Kepler, and Newton, would make astounding strides in physics, astronomy, and mechanics, often building on the insights of Copernicus. How did profoundly religious men such as Copernicus reconcile the insights of reason and observation with loyalty to the church?[261] Many tried to find approaches that would artfully avoid the conflict altogether. These approaches sowed the seeds of the eventual separation of science from theology, as well as from other types of intellectual endeavor. For example, some carefully couched their explorations in instrumental

---

258 *See* DOROTHY STIMSON, THE GRADUAL ACCEPTANCE OF THE COPERNICAN THEORY OF THE UNIVERSE 39 (1917) (citing the Martin Luther quote and explaining its scriptural reference to Joshua 10:10–15).

259 *See* NANCY PEARCEY & CHARLES B. THAXTON, THE SOUL OF SCIENCE: CHRISTIAN FAITH AND NATURAL PHILOSOPHY 37 (Good News Publishers 1994) (noting that while Calvin firmly opposed the Copernican heliocentric world view, he did not attack Copernicus directly in print).

260 *See* TARNAS, *supra* note 253, at 234 and 252 (describing the Protestant reformation and its interplay with scientific revelations).

261 *See* THOMAS S. KUHN, THE COPERNICAN REVOLUTION 197 (1996) (noting that Copernicus was a Catholic cleric who was friendly with members of the Catholic hierarchy).

terms, suggesting that it was simply useful to think about planetary movements in this fashion, regardless of whether there was any ultimate truth to the construction. A preface to Copernicus' major manuscript, inserted without his knowledge, explained that heliocentricity is merely a convenient computational method that should not be taken seriously as a realistic account of the heavens.[262] Not all, however, were willing to adopt the convenient instrumental mantle. For example, when offered the instrumental approach as an escape from the wrath of the inquisition, Galileo eventually declined.[263]

The notion of usefulness is intrinsic to other views of science at this period of time. Science often is more like engineering or problem solving. Understanding the movement of the stars helps ships navigate, for example. It is not necessary to look for the goodness or justice or morality of the movement to benefit from the information. Thus, some tried to define a narrow and limited space for the explorations of science, one that hopefully would not offend or conflict with the Church.

Others tried to avoid conflict by more explicitly delineating separate spheres for science and theology, ones that would implicitly limit the role of the Church. For example, the philosopher and astronomer Giordano Bruno suggested

---

262 *See* TARNAS, *supra* note 253, at 252. Copernicus described his views as the following:

> For it is sufficiently clear that this art is absolutely and profoundly ignorant of the causes of the apparent irregular movements. And if it constructs and thinks up causes—and it has certainly thought up a good many—nevertheless it does not think them up in order to persuade anyone of their truth but only in order that they may provide a correct basis for calculation.

See HAWKING, *supra* note 253.

263 *See* ROSENBERG, *supra* note 216, at 94–95.

that the Bible should be followed for its philosophy rather than its astronomy.[264] Thus, the teachings of both could comfortably coexist. Galileo himself noted that the Church in the past had sanctioned allegorical interpretations of the Bible when its teachings appeared to conflict with scientific evidence.[265]

The Catholic Church initially did not object to Copernicus and his notion of heliocentricity. With Protestant reformers nipping at their heels, however, the Church eventually moved to suppress these emerging areas of science, sometimes with great brutality.[266] As one scholar noted in describing the fate of Bruno, "His stated beliefs that the Bible should be followed for its moral teachings rather than its astronomy, and that all religions and philosophies should coexist in tolerance and mutual understanding . . . received little enthusiasm from the Inquisition."[267]

Although ultimately rejected by the Church, these efforts to avoid conflicts between Church and science would begin the process of creating a separate sphere for science. Science emerged as a realm focusing on understanding nature and the universe through human observation, using theories that the human mind can reason from those observations, and reaching conclusions that can be tested through further

---

264 *See* TARNAS, *supra* note 253, at 253.

265 *See id.* at 259.

266 *See id.* at 251–54 (describing the Catholic Church's original tolerance for Copernican theories and later repression in response to pressure from Protestant reformers).

267 *See id.* at 253; *see also* GIORDANO BRUNO, THE ASH WEDNESDAY SUPPER 126 (Stanley L. Jaki trans., Mouton & Co. 1975) (1584) (explaining that the reason science conflicts with the Bible is because it is too difficult for the masses to understand, so everything was just simplified for their benefit: "the divine lawgiver does not care to speak on that level of truth by which the common folk would not profit").

observations of the universe. It is centered on solving problems and separated from inquiries related to morality and justice. As the observations of science prove more reliable than the revelations of the Church, the separation also enhances reverence for the men of science and their observations. This undermines the authority of the church[268] and further enhances the separation. In other words, as the religious community becomes more chaotic and less reliable, science is becoming more organized.

One could say that the need to separate from theology shaped the scientific sphere. Alternatively, one could say that the two spheres were able to separate because of their differing contours. In either case, it is clear that science settled into a separate space for itself based on observation and confirmation.

The same concepts that separated science from the Church would form the basis of separating science from philosophy.[269] In particular, as science pulled away from theology, philosophers such as Francis Bacon in England and Rene Descartes in Continental Europe began to reconceptualize science and its relationship with both theology and philosophy.[270] They created a distinction between intellectual theories that followed from observation and experimentation and theories that were more remote.[271] The former would be called natural philosophy while the latter

268 *See* TARNAS, *supra* note 253, at 260 (explaining that the Church's refusal to accept Copernicanism and its later expansions caused irreparable harm to the Church's intellectual and spiritual integrity).

269 *See* WOLF, *supra* note 216, at 5–6.

270 *See, e.g.*, GAUKROGER, *supra* note 250, at 116 (describing in detail how Descartes took the Jesuit curriculum that he had studied in his youth, which combined natural philosophy, metaphysics, math, ethics, etc., and separated those fields); *see also* DESCARTES, *supra* note 247.

271 *See* WOLF, *supra* note 216, at 629.

would be called speculative philosophy or some other designation.[272] Most important, natural philosophy should be an objective inquiry, one that is based on reliable methods of inquiry focusing on features that can be quantified.[273]

By the end of the seventeenth century, natural philosophy, which we now call science, had carved out a space for itself strongly differentiated from theology and philosophy. The difference could be identified in terms of the types of questions to explore and the approach to those questions. Science would be an objective inquiry into natural phenomena focusing on solving practical problems and grounded in observation, experimentation, and empirical analysis. This would be distinct from philosophy, which would focus on abstract exploration through human reasoning, and from theology, which would concern spiritual enlightenment through divine revelation.

No sooner does science begin to separate itself out, than others begin to emulate it. This is particularly true in the field of law where some legal thinkers reach out for science almost immediately.

By the late 1600s, Gottfried Wilhelm Leibniz argued that law should be based on natural sciences such as geometry.[274] He created a legal code based on scientific principles intended

---

272 *See id.*

273 *See* KLEMKE, *supra* note 49, at 483–84 (discussing Newtonian science and describing Rene Descartes as the main architect of the epistemological and methodological revolution in science and philosophy).

274 *See* ROGER BERKOWITZ, THE GIFT OF SCIENCE: LEIBNIZ AND THE MODERN LEGAL TRADITION 19 (2005); *see also* M.H. Hoeflich, *Law and Geometry: Legal Science from Leibniz to Langdell*, 30 AM. J. OF LEGAL HIST. 99 (1986) (arguing that Leibniz should be given principle responsibility for developing the geometric paradigm in law). For a detailed description of more modern incarnations of the geometric ideal in legal thought, *see* Thomas C. Grey, *Langdell's Orthodoxy*, 45 U. OF PITT. L. REV. 1, 16–19 (1983).

for adoption throughout the Austro-Hungarian Empire and Europe, although he was unsuccessful in convincing Emperor Leopold I to enact the code.[275] What Leibniz saw in science was more than simply a way of organizing and synthesizing analysis. He saw the possibility of a systematic way of knowing the world, proceeding out of divine and rational first principles.[276] The legal system would operate with an abstract purpose that could be expressed in elemental and reliable theorems. The theorems could be applied to calculate all potential case combinations, allowing legislators to determine all proper outcomes in advance.[277] In this way, law could follow the insights of the science of the time, as it was emerging in a form separate from philosophy and theology.

As described in Chapter IV above, the notion of what constitutes science and what it would mean to make law more scientific will vary across time and among scholars. Nevertheless, law's attraction to science reaches almost back to the time in which science separates itself out from other types of thought. What unites all of these attempts to reach for science is the view that science, in whatever form it takes, can solve the problems of law. Science stands on a pedestal as the "other" that will help law find itself.

It is ironic that science, which did not set out to rival the Church, would shake the Church's foundations by the nineteenth century. Until that time, biology at least remained as a testament to divine creation and direction. Though physics

---

275 *See* BERKOWITZ, *supra* note 86, at 11–12; *see also* DONALD RUTHERFORD, LEIBNIZ AND THE RATIONAL ORDER OF NATURE 240 (Cambridge University Press 1995) (discussing the manifestation of divine wisdom in the physical realm).

276 *See* BERKOWITZ, *supra* note 86, at 19.

277 *See id.* at 35–38 (using Leibniz's combinatorial method for examining contract cases to explore Leibniz's theory of mathematical jurisprudence.)

and astronomy might challenge the notion of a universe created for a purpose by the divine, the complexity, diversity, and adaptation of human and nonhuman biology stood as an argument for the existence of an intelligently designed universe full of purpose and meaning.[278] In other words, until the nineteenth century, biology's complexity served as evidence of the existence of God in the face of the advancing sciences. Biology served that purpose, that is, until the arrival of Charles Darwin. Darwin's theories of evolution and natural selection suggested that finding purpose in nature is illusory.[279] Darwin's work, and that of his contemporaries, showed that the complexity of biology flowed not from the hand of God but from a purely causal process driven by heritable variation and natural selection.[280] This scientific blow would shake the very foundations of religion and religious determinism.

Perhaps the greatest irony, however, is the place of honor and worship to which science has ascended. Science, which had the effect of freeing observation and interpretation from the grasp of the medieval church, looms as its own theocracy within law today.[281] This is certainly not what the men of the scientific revolution intended, nor is it necessarily what modern men and women of science would relish. Our misplaced faith in what some have called "science's ability to

---

278 *See* ROSENBERG, *supra* note 216, at 9 (stating that "[t]he biological realm showed too much complexity, diversity and adaptation to be the product of mere matter in motion; its appearance of design shows the hand of God").

279 *See id.* (stating that Newton and Darwin's theories went "beyond mere determinism by showing all purpose in nature to be illusory").

280 *See id.* at 60.

281 *See supra* Chapters 2–3 (describing internalization and externalization of science in modern law); *cf* Feyeraband, *supra* note 49, at 56 (comparing the broad society's reverence for the judgment of scientists with the reverence once held for Bishops and Cardinals).

answer all questions and displace other ways of knowing"[282] is not imposed from the scientific realm. It is not the men and women of science who have would have science ascend to these lofty heights. Rather, it is our desperation for solutions in law that leads us to place science upon this pedestal.

C. SCIENCE CONFRONTED AND CONFOUNDED

As described earlier, the Scientific Revolution brought both significant advances in science and an important shift in the conceptualization of science. Science emerged from this period as distinct from philosophy, which focused on abstract exploration of topics such as existence and truth, and theology, which focused on spiritual enlightenment.

Of course, science, philosophy, and theology cannot be so neatly distinguished. Despite the conceptual separation of the spheres, the spaces of overlap would challenge the great minds of future generations. Philosophical explorations into the nature of truth, for example, can easily blend into questions relating to determining what information is reliable for science as well as into identifying the proper path for moral and spiritual enlightenment.

To borrow an analogy from science, the three spheres are like water, with its three forms as a liquid, a gas, and a solid. The molecules interact differently within each form,

---

282 *See* ROSENBERG, *supra* note 216, at 7 (describing "scientism" in broader society); *see also* Robert Hollinger, *From Weber to Habermas*, *in* KLEMKE, *supra* note 49, at 546 (noting that Habermas' early work developed a criticism of Weber's adherence to the doctrine of "scientism," which posits that only science is valid and rational and that other disciplines must adopt scientific methods to be considered rational knowledge); *see also* JÜRGEN HABERMAS, TOWARD A RATIONAL SOCIETY: STUDENT PROTEST, SCIENCE, AND POLITICS 64 (Jeremy J. Shapiro trans., Beacon Press 1971).

creating structural variations. Despite these structural differences, there are places of overlap between what counts as one form and what counts as another.[283] In other words, there are circumstances in which the substance is technically water, but it is beginning to behave a lot more like ice. Such is the relationship of science, philosophy, and theology. They are technically distinct, but it is the spaces of overlap that provide some of the most interesting features. It is indeed the spaces of overlap that would eventually confound those who tried to identify what is science in the twentieth century. This period witnessed nothing short of a revolution in thinking about the nature of science and how one should define things scientific.

Across the march of history, different sciences had become separated from philosophy and theology. Astronomy led the way in the sixteenth century, followed by physics in the seventeenth, chemistry in the eighteenth, and finally biology in the nineteenth.[284] Fields of science peeled off, one by one, as they became organized bodies of thought with more distinct boundaries and coherent frames of reference. Identifying these boundaries and determining when a science has fully emerged as a reliable science, rather than something else, however, can be tremendously challenging.

Until the middle of the twentieth century, the notion of what constitutes reliable information in general, and reliable

---

283 For example, at zero degrees Celsius—the freezing point—there is ice. Anywhere above four degrees, it is still water. Beginning at four degrees and going to zero, however, the liquid water begins to behave differently in terms of its density such that it is not really one or the other but something in between.

284 *See* Wolf, *supra* note 216, at 5–6; *see also* Rosenberg, *supra* note 216, at 3 (noting that the history of science from the Greeks to the present is a history of one compartment of philosophy after another breaking away from philosophy and emerging as a separate discipline).

scientific information in particular, was based on the concept of logical positivism. This philosophical framework suggests that statements can be proven true only if they can be confirmed by experience.[285] Truthful statements can be verified through experimentation, quantification, and sensory perception. Only the types of information that are testable through experimentation and observation should be considered the subject of science rather than the subject of philosophy.[286] The logical positivism of the early twentieth century followed a logical tradition stretching back to Descartes and even to forms of Aristotelian thinking.[287] Pressing against the boundaries of this framework, however, philosophers of science in the middle of the century began trying to delineate what kinds of questions we can answer, which might fall within the realm of science, and what kinds of questions we cannot yet answer or will never be able to answer, which might fall within the realm of philosophy.[288] Exploration of these and other questions concerning the definition of science produced a revolution in thinking about the nature of the scientific enterprise.

The revolution began in earnest with the publication of Thomas Kuhn's book, *The Structure of Scientific Revolutions*, which was described some time later as "the single most influential work on the philosophy of science that has been or will be written in this century"[289] and the "most heavily

285 *See* ROSENBERG, *supra* note 216, at 22–23 (describing logical positivism).

286 *See id.* at 23.

287 *See* Ernan McMullin, *Values in Science, in* KLEMKE, *supra* note 49, at 515 (describing the logicist tradition of logical positivism).

288 *See* ROSENBERG, *supra* note 216, at 2–4 (describing the field of philosophy of science and differentiating it from science itself).

289 *See* CLARK GLYMOUR, THEORY AND EVIDENCE 94 (Princeton University Press, 1980) (describing and criticizing the approach launched by Kuhn); *see also* THOMAS S. KUHN, THE STRUCTURE OF SCIENTIFIC REVOLUTIONS (1962).

cited work in the second half of the twentieth century's absorption with science."[290] Kuhn's theories, described in this and later works, engendered a profound soul searching among scientists, or at the very least, a searching look by those who study it. As Kuhn and others challenged the age old vision of science, the smallest, simplest descriptive questions became difficult to answer because they nest inside the larger, more prophetic ones.

Kuhn set out to examine the nature of change in science. How does one fundamental theory give way to another, and what does that tell us about the nature of science? In this endeavor, he separated science into two types of periods: normal science, in which dominant paradigms direct the course of scientific activity; and scientific revolution, in which an established paradigm is supplanted. Kuhn demonstrated that neither of these can support the common notion of scientific activity.

Kuhn's explorations and those that followed exposed enormous gaps in our definitions of science. In fact, they completely undermined philosophy's confidence that it understood anything about science at all.[291] First, the new philosophers of science questioned whether there is any objectivity in science. If one is going to test a hypothesis, for example, how does one know whether that hypothesis successfully passed the test? The choices made when scientists decide whether the available evidence is good enough to warrant acceptance of a hypothesis are themselves value laden.[292] "No puzzle solving enterprise can exist unless its

---

290 *See* Rosenberg, *supra* note 216 at 147.

291 *Id.*

292 *See* Klemke, *supra* note 49, at 490 (describing Rudner); Richard Rudner, *The Scientist* Qua *Scientist Makes Value Judgments, in* Klemke, *supra* note 49, at 492–98.

practitioners share criteria which, for that group and for that time, determine when a particular puzzle has been solved."[293] Distinctions between reliable and unreliable knowledge and between good and bad methods are at least partly value judgments.[294]

Objectivity, says Kuhn, consists not in the correspondence of our theories to the world but in the fact that the members of the scientific community all agree about the theory or ways to evaluate the theory, both of which are completely subjective.[295] Normally, scientists take for granted the background theories of the day and simply try to solve puzzles based on other assumptions and models.[296]

The common view of scientific change is that, scientists, faced with increasing evidence of problems in the observational data, are inspired to search out better explanations. This search leads them to reevaluate the theories that have come before, resulting in a shift. Kuhn and others argue that scientific revolutions generally do not occur this way. First, scientists do not operate in a world of perfection in which observable evidence generally matches available theories. No theory ever fits all the available evidence. Rather, scientists talk about anomalies and recalcitrant instances, looking for ways to refine the prevailing paradigms rather than disposing of them.[297] It would be folly for scientists to operate

---

293 Thomas S. Kuhn, *The Sciences as Problem-Solving Traditions*, *in* CONCEPTIONS OF INQUIRY: A READER 107, 110 (STUART BROWN, JOHN FAUVEL & RUTH FINNEGAN eds., 1981).

294 *See* KLEMKE, *supra* note 49, at 485.

295 *See* THOMAS S. KUHN, THE ESSENTIAL TENSION: SELECTED STUDIES IN SCIENTIFIC TRADITION AND CHANGE 320–39 (1977).

296 *See* CURD ET AL., *supra* note 216, at 67 (describing Kuhn's book, THE STRUCTURE OF SCIENTIFIC REVOLUTIONS, *supra* note 258).

297 *See* Imre Lakatos, *Science and Pseudo-Science*, *in* BROWN, CONCEPTIONS OF INQUIRY, *supra* note 290, at 118 (stating that "scientists talk about anomalies,

otherwise, given that the anomalies themselves may turn out to be erroneous.[298]

In addition, scientists now generally agree that observational evidence cannot prove scientific theories, although that evidence can strongly enhance the probability that the theories are accurate.[299] The problem is that we can never be certain whether we are working from a sufficient amount of observation. For example, Newton's theories of how particles of matter attract other particles of matter are based on observations of planetary movements generalized to all matter in the universe. Our observations, necessarily, are limited to certain bodies during certain periods of time. It is entirely possible, however, that though our observations are correct, our theories are wrong because we simply haven't observed enough matter in the universe to know whether our concept of gravity is accurate or whether entirely different forces are at work.

Others have questioned whether one can ever have faith in observations at all. Most of our scientific observations are

---

recalcitrant instances, not refutations. History of Science, of course, is full of accounts of how crucial experiments allegedly kill theories"); *see also* Thomas Kuhn, *The Sciences as Puzzle-Solving Traditions*, in BROWN, *supra* note 294, at 112 (discussing the importance of unexpected results in defining the astronomical research tradition).

298 *See* Kuhn, *supra* note 293, at 112 (noting that if observations did not match a scientific prediction, a scientist might assume that "the data were at fault: old observations could be re-examined and new measurements made"); *cf.* Lakatos, *supra* note 294, at 118 (stating that "[s]cience is not simply trial and error, a series of conjectures and refutations. 'All swans are white' may be falsified by the discovery of one black swan. But such trivial trial and error does not rank as science").

299 *See* CURD ET AL., *supra* note 216, at 69. The explanation following in the text, using Newton's theories to demonstrate why we can never be certain of scientific theories, is described and set out more fully in CURD ET AL., *supra* note 216, at 69.

not based on direct perception but on scientific instruments. We believe that a particular substance has a particular temperature, but that conclusion is based on the indirect observation of mercury rising in a thermometer rather than any direct observation. What then would count as a direct observation? Perhaps seeing a dog walking across the street would suffice. But then, the sun appears to walk across the sky, and it is an observation that scientists believe to be inaccurate. How then can perception ever be reliable?

Finally, Kuhn pointed out that periods of scientific revolution often challenge the image that science builds carefully on what has gone before, expanding to new horizons as the available evidence increasingly raises questions about the theories that have come before. New theories frequently appear before the old ones have been refuted.[300] In addition, once the revolution occurs, it may require an entire reformulation rather than building upon prior knowledge.[301] Thus, even in times of scientific revolution, science utterly fails to live up to the image of a progressive endeavor, carefully testing established theories and building upon what has come before.

---

300 *See id.* at 67 (describing Kuhn's book, THE STRUCTURE OF SCIENTIFIC REVOLUTIONS, *supra* note 258).

301 *See* KUHN, THE STRUCTURE OF SCIENTIFIC REVOLUTIONS, *supra* note 258, at 98 (describing certain types of revolutionary changes in science and noting that it would be hard to imagine how new theories could arise without this type of destructive changes in belief structures). *See also* CURD ET AL., *supra* note 216, at 227 (explaining Kuhn's denial of cumulativity and the notion that scientific theories are moving closer to some objective theory-independent truth); *see also* Douglas H. Erwin, *Darwin Still Rules, but Some Biologists Dream of a Paradigm Shift*, N.Y. TIMES, June 27, 2007, *available at* http://www.nytimes.com/2007/06/26/science/26essay.html?_r=1&ref=science&oref=slogin (suggesting that the Darwinian notion of selection may soon be replaced by a new paradigm of evolution based on mutation).

Others attacked the notion that our scientific theories are reliably structured from empirical observation. Sciences operate by making generalizations from directly observable items or even from nonobservable items such as electrons.[302] As Popper pointed out, no rule can ever guarantee that a generalization, even one inferred from a direct observation, is true.[303] No matter how true that observation may be, the generalization may be misguided. Induction, therefore, is a myth.[304]

Even observation itself may be unreliable. Not only do available instruments limit it, the experiences that we bring to the observation shape it and our cultural expectations influence it. As one author eloquently explained: "Contrast the freshman's view of college with that of his ancient tutor. Compare a man's first glance at the motor of his car with a similar glance ten exasperating years later."[305] The items examined are the same, and yet we interpret them differently based on experience and expectations.

To some extent, these arguments can be countered by the notion that we should be able to control for these variations by designing something consistent to observe and by factoring out our individual distortions. Although a wonderful

---

302 *See* Ruse, *supra* note 209, at 72–73; *see also* Toulmin, *supra* note 210, at 358, 359–360 (discussing whether a neutrino "exists" and what it would take to prove or produce it).

303 *See* Karl R. Popper, *Philosophy of Science: A Personal Report*, *in* BRITISH PHILOSOPHY IN THE MID-CENTURY 155, 167 (C.A. Mace ed., 1957) (stating that "we can say that theories can never be inferred from observational statements, or rationally justified by them.").

304 *See* Popper, *supra* note 303, at 166 (agreeing with Hume's proposition that "there can be no valid logical argument allowing us to establish 'that those instances, of which we have had no experience, resemble those, of which we have had experience'").

305 *See* N. R. Hanson, *Observation*, *in* KLEMKE, *supra* note 49, at 345.

concept in theory, the new philosophers of science challenged the notion that human beings are ever capable of such unsullied thought, freezing from one's mind the influences arising from one's personal experiences and from the subtle perspectives of the scientific community.[306]

I would call these philosophers scientific subjectivists.[307] Scientific subjectivists argued that the prevailing definition of science as a reliable method of testing and organizing society's knowledge and building upon that knowledge, simply cannot stand up to a rigorous examination. As with many deconstructionist movements, however, the problem is that while the new philosophy devastated the prevailing view of what science is, it created no other definition of what science could be. Most important, it left no coherent way to distinguish science from nonscience. If science is not what we think it is, how can it claim to be any different from astrology or theology or even magic?

A number of philosophers from the twentieth century tried to construct alternative definitions of what constitutes science. Popper, for example, suggested that the hallmark of true science is falsification. Those advancing a particular theory should be able to specify in advance something that the theory could predict and for which the theorist would be willing to abandon the theory if the prediction failed.[308]

---

306 For extreme examples of this phenomenon, *see* Fritz Machlup, *Are the Social Sciences Really Inferior?, in* KLEMKE, *supra* note 49, at 135, 138–39 (noting that German mathematicians and physicists rejected Jewish what they considered Jewish theorems such as Einstein's relativity and Russian biologists stuck to a inaccurate mutations theory due to politics); *see also* ROSENBERG, *supra* note 216, at 163–64 (describing feminist and race theory critiques of science).

307 This is not a term found in philosophy of science literature, but I believe it captures the essence of their perspectives.

308 *See* Lakatos, *supra* note 297, at 117–18 (describing Popper).

A science should be able to make risky predictions, ones that we would not expect without the theory.[309] Falsification sounds like a good bedrock principle for a science, but it was a failure itself. As Thagard points out, the falsification principle either ruled out most of science as unscientific or ruled out nothing.[310]

The falsification principle has been battered into the ground across time, so I will only describe a few of the refutations here.[311] First, it is simply not the case that any theories agree with all of the observable facts.[312] As the Nobel Prize recipient Francis Crick noted, "[a]ny theory that fits all the facts is bound to be wrong, since some of the facts will be misleading or just wrong in themselves."[313] One cannot abandon a theory whenever it makes a false prediction

309 *See* Popper, *supra* note 303, at 159 (arguing that confirmations of a theory should only count if "they are the result of *risky predictions*, that is to say, if, unenlightened by the theory in question, we should have expected an event incompatible with the theory—an event that would have refuted the theory").

310 *See* Thagard, *supra* note 50, at 225; *cf.* ROSENBERG, *supra* note 216, at 137 (noting that science cannot live up to its own definition of rigor).

311 *See* Thagard, *supra* note 50 (explaining that the vicissitudes of the verification principles are well known); Larry Lauden, *Commentary: Science at the Bar—Causes for Concern*, 7 SCIENCE, TECH. & HUM. VALUES no. 41, 16, 18 (Fall 1982) (noting that numerous authors have shown that the requirements of testability, revisability, and falsification are exceedingly weak requirements).

312 *See* Philipp G. Frank, *The Variety of Reasons for the Acceptance of Scientific Theories, in* KLEMKE, *supra* note 49, at 465 (noting that it has never happened that all conclusions drawn from a theory have agreed with the observable facts).

313 *See* Frank Barlow, *Introduction to* WIDO, THE CARMEN DE HASTINGAE PROELIO OF GUY, BISHOP OF AMIEN xl (Frank Barlow trans., Oxford University Press 1999) (quoting Francis Crick).

because science is a complicated undertaking and one cannot know if the falsification itself is correct.[314]

In addition, everything that we think of as science could be falsified yet still be true. For example, if we reenact Newton's apple scenario and the apple drifts away instead, the observation does not necessarily refute the laws of gravity. Some other force may have been in operation at the time.[315]

Most important, although Popper's falsification principle was intended to distinguish between science and pseudo-science, falsification does not describe the way scientists actually operate. If science is about what we perceive and what we can verify, the definition seems to leave out a lot of how science has actually operated and what scientists do. As Lakatos pointed out, "[h]ad Popper ever asked a Newtonian scientist under what experimental conditions he would abandon Newtonian theory, some Newtonian scientists would have been exactly as nonplussed as are some of the Marxists."[316]

To some extent, the works of those such as Popper arose out of a desire to separate what they saw as true science from pretenders to the throne, including Marxism, Freudianism, and astrology.[317] This orientation hampers the enterprise.

---

314 *See* CURD ET AL., *supra* note 216, at 64 (noting the abandonment problem); Wolpert, *supra* note 212, at 295 (noting that falsifications may be wrong).

315 *See* Kitcher, *supra* note 90, at 87 (describing the Newton apple scenario and its influence on the falsifiability principle).

316 *See* Lakatos, *supra* note 294, at 118.

317 *See* Popper, *supra* note 300, at 157 (explaining that he felt "these other three theories [Marxist history, psychoanalysis, and individual psychology] posed as sciences while in fact they were of the character of primitive myths rather than of science; that they resembled astrology rather than astronomy"); *see also* Thagard, *supra* note 50, at 229 (describing the decline of astrology—once held to be a science—to the status of an unpromising

Definitions crafted with an eye toward distinguishing particular examples become less workable as general rules. Nevertheless, others following Popper have been equally unable to delineate a coherent definition of what constitutes science. The definitions proposed have proven incapable of separating astronomy from astrology[318] or creation science from evolution.[319] Part of the problem flows from inconsistent visions of what we are trying to define. For example, are we adopting a normative view or a descriptive view? In other words, is this what science is or what science at its best ought to be?

Moreover, in trying to define science, are we talking about (a) a method of obtaining information, (b) the information gained from that method, or (c) the intent of those engaging in the method? Different definitions of science seem variously grounded in each. For some, the objectivity of science refers to the truth and character of the information obtained; for others, the objectivity of science refers to the reliability of the method.[320] Still others identify science in ways that seem to focus on the intent of those who

---

project, and eventually, a pseudoscience); Carl G. Hempel, *Two Basic Types of Scientific Explanation*, *in* CURD, ET AL., *supra* note 216, at 685–94 (comparing Deductive and Probabilistic explanations and pointing to Freud's vagueness in support of the notion that psychoanalysis is not a science).

318 *See* PATRICK GRIM, PHILOSOPHY OF SCIENCE AND THE OCCULT 15 (SUNY Press 1983) (noting that most philosophers take astrology as a "prime example of a pseudo-science . . . however much they may disagree as to precisely *why* astrology is pseudo-scientific or as precisely what astrology's faults are" (emphasis in original)).

319 *See* Laudan, *supra* note 311, at 17 (arguing that in declaring creationism non scientific, a federal trial court may have reached the right result but for unsupportable reasons).

320 *See* HELEN E. LONGINO, SCIENCE AS SOCIAL KNOWLEDGE: VALUES & OBJECTIVITY IN SCIENTIFIC INQUIRY 63 (1990) (explaining that those who believe science provides objectivity use two different senses of the word).

practice the art. For example, some scholars speak of science as the attainment of truth and the pursuit of knowledge, or at least the closest possible realization of that.[321] These confusions contribute to the great muddle of trying to define science.

This frustrating exercise has created a tendency toward extremes, even among scientists themselves. When pressed to abandon the notion of science as certain and infallible, some scientists shift to a forlorn skepticism, viewing their endeavors as no more than a game played with arbitrary rules or an enterprise based ultimately on faith.[322] Some philosophers go even further, suggesting that we abandon the idea of science as a separate or privileged domain of inquiry and recognize it as no different from any other set of myths or beliefs.[323]

Bruno Latour, a philosopher of science, describes a striking example of this phenomenon in the opening of his book, *Essays on the Reality of Science Studies*.[324] In dramatic prose, Latour recounts his experience at a conference in which a scientist quietly took him aside and, after taking a deep breath, asked him, "Do you believe in reality?" and "Do we [scientists] know more than we used to?"[325] Through this and other conversations, Latour came to understand that scientists viewed what he had always thought of as adding realism to science as a threat to the very calling of science. Latour was shocked. "How could this misunderstanding

321 *See, e.g.*, KLEMKE, *supra* note 49, at 31.

322 Kitcher, *supra* note 90, at 80 (describing philosopher George Berkeley's use of the term "forlorn skepticism" and expanding on the way scientists react to challenges by philsophers of science).

323 *See* Wolpert, *supra* note 212, at 289.

324 The following episode is recounted in BRUNO LATOUR, PANDORA'S HOPE: ESSAYS ON THE REALITY OF SCIENCE STUDIES 2–3 (1999).

325 *See* LATOUR, *supra* note 324, at 2.

come about? How could I have lived long enough to be asked in all seriousness this incredible question, 'Do you believe in reality?'"[326]

D. AN UNEASY TRUCE

To answer the question what is science is almost as presumptuous as to try to state the meaning of life itself.

Lewis Wolpert[327]

Retreating from the edges of oblivion and despair, philosophers of science have settled into an uneasy truce. After all, as Lewis Wolpert points out, applications of science to technologies such as electronics and jet airplanes should give us some confidence that reality is involved in the enterprise of science, even if we cannot definitively identify the boundaries of that enterprise.[328] The approach begins with a certain awe and humility, a recognition of the difficulty of defining science at all. With this in mind, a number of scholars have proposed various groupings of elements that would delineate science from nonscience endeavors. The elements are intended to roughly represent shared values of the scientific community.

One cannot overemphasize the imperfection of the endeavor. No elements, either individually or as a group, can accurately separate what we think of as science from nonscience. Nevertheless, on the whole, these criteria give some comfort that an approach or a conclusion is more likely than not to fall within what we consider science.

---

326 LATOUR, *supra* note 324, at 3.

327 John Ziman, *What is Science?, in* KLEMKE, *supra* note 49, at 48.

328 REECE, *supra* note 53, at ix.

Various scholars would choose different elements for the group. Some would suggest five elements, others three, and still others nine.[329] These elements would apply to test both whether a field can be called science and whether individual theories within the field are reasonably scientific. As a general matter, the approaches focus on the following types of issues. First, are they testable in the sense that they able to be tested? In other words, are they based on observations from the physical world that can be quantified and independently verified.

Second, do they have predictive capacity? In other words, are they not just capable of being tested but are they also capable of making predictions that we can test for accuracy and consistency of the theories. Although Popper's falsifiability principle no longer stands as the sole hallmark of a true science, it is still useful to consider whether a science or a theory can be put to the test of prediction. For example, our sticks and elephants could be tested by halting the sticks and waiting for the elephants to rampage.[330] Third, how

---

329 *See* THOMAS S. KUHN, THE ESSENTIAL TENSION: SELECTED STUDIES IN SCIENTIFIC TRADITION AND CHANGE 322 (1977) (listing accuracy, consistency, scope, simplicity, and fruitfulness.); Machlup, *supra* note 303, at 136 (listing invariability of observations, objectivity of observations and explanations, verifiability of hypotheses, exactness of findings, measurability of phenomena, constancy of numerical relationships, predictability of future events, distance from everyday experience, standards of admissions and requirements); KLEMKE, *supra* note 49, at 32 (adapting Herbert Feigl's suggestions to come up with intersubjective testability, reliability, definiteness and precision, coherence or systematic character, and comprehensiveness or scope); Thagard, *supra* note 50, at 31–32 (nesting the various elements into 3 broad groupings related to theory, community, and historical context); *see also* CURD ET AL., *supra* note 216, at 228–30 (describing Kuhn's five shared epistemic values).

330 *See supra* text accompanying note 209–10 (describing the sticks and elephants story).

comprehensive are they? Do they explain things that other theories have been unable to explain, and do they pull together disparate threads of the particular field or even a group of fields? Watson and Crick's discovery of DNA, for example, also explained the fundamental laws of Mendelian genetics, that is, how hereditary traits travel from generation to generation.[331]

Fourth, are they fruitful? Do they give rise to other new theories that continue to advance the understanding of the field or are the theories focused on accommodating known facts?[332] This is a variation on the notion of progressivity. In other words, are they the foundation upon which new things can be built. And finally, following a long-held principle of science, are they simple? Are they elegant and parsimonious or do they require us to take many mental detours to follow them? A variation on this theme is the notion of whether they are understandable given what we think we can rely on. Do they follow common sense or do they require us to substantially suspend our disbelief?

It is critical to understand that all these elements have significant weaknesses for defining science. Though it is important to base scientific theory on observations from the physical world, science is frequently incomplete. Thagard pointed out, for example, that there was no physical foundation for the continental drift theory when it was proposed, and yet it has become an important part of geologic science.[333]

Similarly, predictive capacity is important, but it is no guarantee of the accuracy of a theory. The theory may simply

---

331 *See* ROSENBERG, *supra* note 216, at 77.

332 *See* LAKATOS, *supra* note 297, at 24–25 (comparing Newtonian science with Marxism).

333 *See* Thagard, *supra* note 50, at 68.

be based on the wrong underlying concepts. For example, some acupuncture approaches are based on the notion of rerouting the forces of the "chi" of the human body.[334] Suppose that acupuncture turns out to be effective for a reason entirely unrelated to any notion of chi—a useful therapy with a nonuseful explanation. In that case, the field might have predictive capacity and yet still be inaccurate. Moreover, not all valuable scientific theories are predictive, and certainly not at the time of their inception. The Copernican theories were far better at explanation than prediction.[335]

A theory that is comprehensive and can pull together a number of threads is particularly valuable, but lack of comprehensiveness should not disqualify something. As Grover Maxwell explained, the scientist who theorizes that invisible bugs called "crobes" may be making us sick would not be able to explain all disease processes but would still have made an important and scientifically valid contribution.[336] Finally, simplicity and common sense remain desirable qualities of good science. Nevertheless, these values cannot always be satisfied in science. One has to suspend a great deal of disbelief to understand particle and wave theory, not to mention the notion that the earth moves around the sun.[337]

---

334 *See* STUX, BERMAN, & POMERANZ, BASICS OF ACUPUNCTURE 87 (K.A. Sahm trans., Springer 5th ed. 2003).

335 *See* Ernan McMullin, *Rationality and Paradigm Change in Science, in* PAUL HORWICH, WORLD CHANGES: THOMAS KUHN AND THE NATURE OF SCIENCE 35, 74, 55–78 (1993).

336 *See* Grover Maxwell, *The Ontological Status of Theoretical Entities, in* KLEMKE, *supra* note 49, at 363–65 (responding to Toulmin's hypothetical scientist who theorizes the existence of "crobes"); *see also* text accompanying note 210 (describing Toulmin's hypothetical).

337 *See* Frank, *supra* note 256, at 468–69 (noting that Copernican theories were not only nonnatural but were a serious violation of the rule to keep principles of science as close to common sense as possible).

On the whole, the vision of science among scientists and philosophers of science is framed as an effort to understand what is real and true in an enduring sense. The effort may be imperfect, limited as it must necessarily be by the imperfect beings who engage in the process. We may have difficulty recognizing what is true in the world around us. In fact, we may be entirely incapable of recognizing it, but that does not mean the reality does not exist. There is circularity in science because what we define as the way to take us there and how we determine when we get there are both subjective, but that is different from the question of whether there is a "there" to get to.

Most important, the effort of science still aims at building on the knowledge that has come before, testing new theories that can better incorporate what we know. It is a progressive effort that helps us move toward an ever deeper and more meaningful understanding of the world around us.

Throughout this process, however, it is critical to recognize weaknesses in the notion that the method of obtaining information necessarily dictates the truth of the results. A theory may appear through induction, intuition, or pure guess. Myths may contain kernels of truth and scientific theory may have much nonsense in it.[338] Proper scientific method or lack thereof does not necessarily speak to the

338 *See* Popper, *supra* note 303, at 162 (noting that all or very nearly all scientific theories originate from myths); *see also* Thagard, *supra* note 50, at 68 (noting that medicine and chemistry had magical origins); Lakatos, *supra* note 297, at 115 (noting that a statement may be pseudoscientific even if it is eminently plausible and everybody believes in it and it may be scientifically valuable even if it is unbelievable and nobody believes it given that something may be of supreme scientific value even if no one understand it, let alone believes in it).

value of the insight, although proper scientific method can certainly help test the theory proposed.[339]

Even in terms of testing theories, modern scientists do not claim that their theories are true. Rather, they speak of a theory as being "well supported" or "rationally acceptable."[340] When scientists say that they accept a theory, they may mean that they believe that the theory is the best supported of the available alternatives or that it offers the most fruitful possibilities for research in the immediate future.[341] The most we hope for in science isn't proof of truth or falsehood but some confidence that the hypothesis is true more likely than not or perhaps just useful given what we know at the moment.[342] This is not at all what law dreams of when it reaches for science to solve our problems. It is hard to imagine putting someone in jail on the basis that the evidence is the best we have at the moment and makes somewhat more sense than the available alternatives.

---

339 *See* KLEMKE, *supra* note 49, at 35 (describing newer visions of science in light of Popper's criticisms).

340 *See* McMullin, *supra* note 287, at 519.

341 *Id.* at 520.

342 *See* KLEMKE, *supra* note 49, at 402. Interestingly, this movement away from determinism mirrors recent developments in math and physics. In quantum physics, for example, the question of whether a single proton will emit an alpha particle at a particular time is a question of probabilities. For a description of these scientific advancements and their implications for philosophy of science, *see* ROSENBERG, *supra* note 216, at 9–11.

CHAPTER VII

Misunderstanding the Limits of Science

The revolution in modern views of science seems to have gone largely unnoticed in law. Judges and legal scholars do talk about what counts as "good" science.[343] There is no

343 *See, e.g.*, Frye v. United States, 293 F. 1013, 1014 (D.C. Cir. 1923) (holding that a scientific technique "must be sufficiently established to have gained general acceptance in the particular field in which it belongs" to be admissible as the basis for expert testimony); Daubert v. Merrell Dow Pharmaceuticals, Inc., 509 U.S. 579, 590 (stating that "in order to qualify as 'scientific knowledge,' an inference or assertion must be derived by the scientific method. Proposed testimony must be supported by appropriate validation—i.e., 'good grounds,' based on what is known."); *cf.* Kumho Tire Company, Ltd. v. Carmichael, 526 U.S. 137, 150 (1999) (noting that the *Daubert* factors for establishing admissibility of expert testimony of scientific techniques are not a "definitive checklist or test"); *see also* In re Joint Eastern & Southern Dist. Asbestos Litig., 52 F.3d 1124 (2d Cir. 1995) (discussing epidemiological and clinical evidence of causation in products liability action against manufacturer of asbestos-containing product); U.S. v. Velasquez, 64 F.3d 844 (3d Cir. 1995) (examining expert testimony regarding forensic handwriting analysis in drug prosecution); State v. Buckner,

mention, however, of the fact that we might not be able to define what science is at all, at least not in a way that definitively separates it from nonscience.

Failure to understand the limitations of science creates tremendous distortions when we try to make law more scientific or to let scientists solve our legal issues. From one perspective, the problem plays out as a misuse of science and scientific information.[344] Science begins with observations and theories that are rationally acceptable and well supported, which is something far less than certain and infallible. Ignoring these qualifications, law tries to translate science into social and legal conclusions without understanding the perils of that translation.[345]

941 P.2d 667 (Wash. 1997) (discussing statistical probability evidence based upon DNA profiling in murder prosecution); Bert Black, *Science and the Law in the Wake of Daubert: A New Search for Scientific Knowledge*, 72 TEX. L. REV. 715 (1994) (providing a pragmatic account of what separates science from other forms of knowledge); Michael J. Saks, *The Aftermath of Daubert: An Evolving Jurisprudence of Expert Evidence*, 40 JURIMETRICS J. 229 (2000) (examining the developing jurisprudence of expert evidence under the Federal Rules of Evidence in post-Daubert scientific evidence cases).

344 *See generally* DAVID L. FAIGMAN, LEGAL ALCHEMY: THE USE AND MISUSE OF SCIENCE IN THE LAW (1999); *see also* DAVID L. FAIGMAN, LABORATORY OF JUSTICE: THE SUPREME COURT'S 200-YEAR STRUGGLE TO INTEGRATE SCIENCE AND THE LAW, 203–04 (2004) (noting that scientific facts have the "frustrating tendency to change, either because our understanding of them changes or the facts themselves change in an evolving and technologically advancing society . . . [and that] attaching constitutional principles to disputed or changeable facts can be expected to create greater difficulties and more controversy.").

345 *See* JASANOFF, *supra* note 52, at xiii–xiv (1995) (noting that scientific claims, especially those that are implicated in legal controversies, are contingent on particular localized circumstances and freighted with buried presumptions).

A. PROBLEMS IN TRANSLATION

Misuse of science creates concerns on several levels. First, one might worry whether legal actors are good scientists. When judges rely on a scientific study as part of an opinion, do they have the capacity to read the data properly? When legal academics engage in their own empirical analyses, do they design the study properly, code the data in a reasonable manner, and interpret the results in a supportable fashion?

Consider various applications of the brain scan imaging technology known as fMRI.[346] The technology measures blood flow in the brain, observing increases to different brain segments as subjects engage in various activities or discussion of different types of issues.[347] Advocates of brain imaging technology have high hopes for its application in the field of law, from more mundane applications such as determining whether a suspect is lying to more difficult applications such as predicting future violent behavior to truly esoteric inquiries such as understanding the human motivations around which law should be designed and measuring those deeply shared beliefs upon which legal systems should be based.[348] On the more basic front, organizations have

346 *See* Hank Greely & Judy Illes, *NeuroScience-Based Lie Detection: The Urgent Need for Regulation*, 33 AM J.L. & MED. 377, 384 (2007) (discussing the implications of using fMRI data in legal contexts); *see generally* Stephen J. Morse, *Brain Overclaim Syndrome and Criminal Responsibility: The Urgent Need for Regulation*, 3 OHIO ST. J. CRIM. L. 397 (2006) (discussing the risk of overvaluation of the potential for neuroscience to resolve questions of legal responsibility).

347 *See* Greely & Illes, *supra* note 346, at 380–81 (discussing the measurement of blood-oxygenation-level dependent contrast to measure neural activity).

348 *See, e.g.*, Stephen J. Morse, *Brain Overclaim Syndrome and Criminal Responsibility: A Diagnostic Note*, 3 OHIO ST. J. CRIM. L. 397 (2006) (criticizing over enthusiasm for the use of brain imaging studies in the context of determining criminal responsibility); Hank Greely & Judy Illes, *NeuroScience-Based Lie*

begun offering fMRI-based lie-detection services, with one claiming to have a current accuracy rate of 93 percent with an expected accuracy rate of 99 percent when development of the product is complete.[349]

Proper interpretation of such data will be tremendously challenging for the legal system, both in terms of understanding the data itself and in terms of recognizing the limitations of the conclusions one can draw from the data. As a general matter, brain scan imaging at the moment is expensive and requires cooperative subjects.[350] Brain scan data reliability has other limitations as well. Scientific testing has taken place in controlled settings with the explorations directed at narrow and limited inquiries.[351] Applying that technology in real-world settings would require overcoming enormous challenges.[352] In the lie-detector setting, for example, simple movements of the head or jaw can make the data unreadable.[353] In addition, there are suggestions that subjects may be able to render the results unreliable through well-rehearsed lies.[354] In the context of testing to see what areas of the brain are activated during a given activity, simply

---

Detection: The Urgent Need for Regulation, 33 AM J.L. & MED. 377 (2007) (criticizing fMRI-based lie-detection services); *see also supra* text accompanying note 2 (citing *New York Times* article extolling the potential of fMRI technology).

349 *See* Greely & Illes, *supra* note 346, at 390, 392.

350 *See* Morse, *supra* note 346, at 403.

351 *See* Greely & Illes, *supra* note 346, at 402–05 (discussing the shortcomings of current fMRI lie-detection methodology); *See* Morse, *supra* note 345, at 403.

352 *Cf.* Robin Feldman, *Considerations on the Emerging Implementation of Biometric Technology*, 25 HASTINGS COMM. & ENT. L.J. 653, 662–65 (2003) (discussing the challenges of applying biometric identification technologies, such as facial imaging and retinal scanning, in real world settings).

353 Greely & Illes, *supra* note 346, at 404–05.

354 *Id.*

thinking about other things may activate other areas of the brain in ways that interfere with reliability of the data.[355] As a law enforcement tool, such information has severe limitations.

Brain scan and other neurological data also are offered in support of various legal doctrines, particularly those related to treating adolescents differently from the way in which we treat adults for purposes ranging from criminal liability to medical consent.[356] There may be very good reasons for treating adolescents differently from adults, but the neurological studies presented as additional support for these policies are insufficient to support the propositions for which they are offered.[357]

Part of the problem when legal actors try to apply this type of research lies in understanding the difference between

---

355 *See id.*

356 *See, e.g.,* Morse, *supra* note 346, at 408–09 (describing presentation of neuroscience data concerning application of the death penalty to adolescents in the case of Roper v. Simmons, 543 U.S. 551 (2005)); William Gardner, David Scherer & Maya Tester, *Asserting Scientific Authority: Cognitive Development and Adolescent Legal Rights,* 44 AM. PSYCHOLOGIST 895, 897 (1989) (discussing studies applying scientific knowledge to competence to consent, generally in accord with the observation that "there is no basis for differentiation of adolescents from adults on the ground of competence alone." (quoting G. Melton, *Toward "personhood" for Adolescents: Autonomy and Privacy as Values in Public Policy,* 38 AM. PSYCHOLOGIST 99–103 (1983)). Research does indicate, however, that adolescents are competent to participate in the decision-making process. *See, e.g.,* Lois A. Weithorn & Susan B. Campbell, *The Competency of Children and Adolescents to Make Informed Treatment Decisions,* 53 CHILD DEV. 1589, 1596 (1982) (finding that adolescents were competent to make medical decisions concerning their own health care based on empirical research, and that children as young as 9 years old were capable of comprehending what is required of them when stating a preference for treatment); *cf.* Bersoff, *supra* note 376 (describing the misuse of survey data concerning adolescents in the school prayer case of Lee v. Weisman, 112 S. Ct. 2649 (1992)).

357 *See supra* sources cites at note 353.

finding a statistically significant result and finding a result that will hold true in all cases or even almost all cases.[358] For example, imagine that we are testing the hypothesis that subjects who are lying will light up what we designate as the red portion of the brain during a scan. The study will compare an experimental group and a control group. A valid study, properly designed, might find that those who are lying light up the red portion of the brain in a way that is statistically significant over those in the control group. There will, however, be significant overlap in the results. Some in the control group will have had red-portion brain activity and some in the group of people who were lying will have had no red-portion activity.

The notion of statistical significance is itself a misleading concept. Although certainly not a problem in the small-scale brain scan studies, given a large enough sample, even minor differences will result in a finding of statistical significance.[359] A frequent error in social science is to confuse finding a statistically significant difference with finding that the difference is important.[360] If social scientists fall prey to this error, one should not be surprised to see the problem magnified when social science research reaches the courts.

Most important, finding brain correlations is only a tiny part of understanding the complexities of why that brain activity is occurring. As one scholar noted:

> Discovering the neural correlates of mental phenomena does not tell us how these phenomena are possible. . . . For example,

358 The hypothetical explained in this paragraph is derived from an excellent explanation in Morse, *supra* note 346, at 403–04.

359 *See* John R. Allison & Thomas W. Sager, *Valuable Patents Redux: On the Enduring Merit of using Patent Characteristics to Identify Valuable Patents,* 85 TEX. L. REV. 1719, 1779 (2007).

360 *See* Allison & Sager, *supra* note 356, at 1779.

> the brains of late adolescents are almost certainly the same around the globe—holding nutrition and the like constant—but the rates of behaviors associated with immature adolescent brains, such as impulsive criminality, vary widely from place to place and from time to time. Monolithic brain explanation of complex behavior is almost always radically incomplete.[361]

Despite these limitations, legal actors are tempted to draw dramatic conclusions from the results of brain scan data. I saw a classic example of this in a recent talk given by a young scholar. The scholar was discussing the law's refusal to treat gifts the same way it treats other types of voluntary contracts and the notion that law should not interfere in some types of personal interactions to avoid tainting the emotional content of those behaviors. The scholar excitedly pointed to fMRI technology showing that when people give gifts, their reactions involve the same portion of the brain that appears to be active when people receive rewards. Thus, gifts should be treated in the same way as other self-interested transactions because the emotional content is analogous.

This is a tremendous leap from a tiny amount of data. The fact that blood flow increases in the same general area of the brain during two activities tells us very little about what is occurring, let alone about the emotional influence of the actions. It certainly does not give us enough information upon which we can build a legal regime.

In the case of data presented in a court setting, one might expect the court system to be able to filter out data and technologies that are not sufficiently reliable or relevant to the question at hand. The tests for admissibility of scientific evidence are framed by a very old case, *Frye*, and a newer

---

361 Morse, *supra* note 346, at 404.

case *Daubert*.[362] In 1923, the Federal District Court for the District of Columbia in the *Frye* case confirmed a murder conviction, rejecting the defendant's contention that he should have been permitted to introduce evidence of a polygraph test. The *Frye* opinion set the standard, subsequently adopted in federal courts and in many state courts, that scientifically based expert testimony should only be admitted if the expert's opinion was developed using methods generally accepted in the relevant professional community.[363]

In 1993, the Supreme Court addressed the issue of expert testimony in a case concerning the admissibility of epidemiological studies to support a claim of birth defects from the antinausea drug Bendectin. The Court cast aside the *Frye* test and its general admissibility standard for the federal courts, ruling that the Federal Rules of Evidence superseded the test.[364] Applying the Federal Rules, the Court determined that the task for judges faced with scientifically based evidence is to determine whether the evidence is scientifically valid and whether it can be properly applied to the facts at issue.[365] The *Daubert* opinion then set out a list of factors to be considered, including whether it has been subjected to peer review and publication; the known error rate;

---

362 *See* Frye v. United States, 293 F. 1013, 1014 (D.C. Cir. 1923) (holding that a scientific technique must be generally accepted by the relevant field to be admissible as the basis of an expert's opinion); *cf.* Daubert v. Merrill Dow Pharmaceuticals, 509 U.S. 579, 592–96 (1993) (outlining factors a court might weigh in determining admissibility of expert testimony based on scientific techniques).

363 *See* MURRAY LEVINE, LEAH WALLACH, & DAVID LEVINE, PSYCHOLOGICAL PROBLEMS, SOCIAL ISSUES, AND THE LAW 40 (2d ed. 2007) (describing *Frye* and its widespread adoption).

364 *See* Daubert, 509 U.S. at 587.

365 *See* Daubert, 509 U.S. at 592–93.

and the existence and maintenance of control standards.[366] Finally, the Court noted that what it described as the more rigid test of general acceptance no longer applies, although the idea underlying the general acceptance test could have a bearing in the guise of whether the theory proffered had obtained widespread acceptance.[367]

In theory, standards like the one in *Daubert* could serve to filter evidence that is unreliable as a matter of methodology or as a matter of application to the facts of the case. The results, however, have been quite different. Almost all courts applying the *Daubert* standard have adopted tremendously liberal standards of admission, relying on cross-examination to expose weaknesses and allowing the fact finder to assess the weight that should be accorded the evidence.[368]

---

366 *See id.* at 593–94.

367 *See id.* at 594.

368 LEVINE ET AL., *supra* note 360, at 43; *see also* P.D. Blanck & H.M. Berven, *Evidence of Disability After Daubert*, 5 PSYCHOL. PUB. POL'Y & L. 16 (1999); J. P. Lipton, *The Use and Acceptance of Social Science in Business Litigation after Daubert*, 5 PSYCHOL., PUB. POL'Y & L. 59 (1999); D.W. Shuman, *The Psychology of Deterrence in Tort Law*, 42 KANSAS L. REV. 115 (1993); C.L. Studebaker & J. Goodman-Delahunty, *Expert Testimony in the Courts: The Influence of the Daubert, Joiner, and Kumho Decisions,* 8 PSYCHOL. PUB. POL'Y & L. 139 (2002). *Daubert* and its progeny have received their share of criticism. *See* Daubert v. Merrell Dow Pharmaceuticals, Inc., 509 U.S. 579, 598–601 (1993) (Rehnquist, J., dissenting) (criticizing the majority's holding as obliging judges to adopt a role as "amateur scientists"); *see also* Andrew R. Stolfi, *Why Illinois Should Abandon Frye's General Acceptance Standard for the Admission of Novel Scientific Evidence,* 78 CHI. KENT. L. REV. 861, 894–95 (2003) (noting and discussing criticisms of *Daubert* arguing that *Frye* provides a better standard based on the assumptions that "first, scientists are the proper authorities to gauge the scientific validity of a technique or method; second, general acceptance of a scientific technique or method equates scientific validity; and third, scientific validity equals evidentiary reliability."); *cf.* Hon. Daniel P. Ryan, *Expert Testimony and Scientific Evidence: Does M.C.L. 600.2955 "Assist" the Trial Judge in Michigan Tort Cases?,* 75 U. DET. MERCY L. REV. 263, 304 (1998) (arguing that "the Michigan

Tests such as *Daubert* also theoretically could allow actors in the legal system to begin to understand the limitation of science and scientific evidence, as cross-examination explored the uncertainty of any given data. Jurors, however, demonstrate extreme deference to scientific evidence and experts, ignoring weaknesses and generally assuming its relevance.

Jurors are not alone in being mesmerized and misled by scientific evidence. Legal history is replete with examples of courts misusing scientific evidence or crediting pseudo-scientific evidence. Classic examples include *Brown v. Board of Education*,[369] *Muller v. Oregon*, and *Ballew v. Georgia*.[370] In *Muller* the Supreme Court upheld limitations on the number of hours that women could work in a day on the grounds that their "special physical organization" makes them particularly susceptible to the dangers of long work hours.[371] The Court relied on the famous Brandeis Brief, which gathered evidence from domestic and foreign sources purporting to demonstrate, among other things, differences in women's physical constitution that required provisions for their particular health and safety.[372] The supposed empirical evidence, however, consisted primarily of broad value-laden statements supported largely by casual observation and

legislature may have selected a narrower standard than Daubert in an attempt to avoid the criticism that the Supreme Court had in its own opinion regarding this particular "general consideration" for its potential lack of reliability.")

369 *See* Brown v. Board of Ed., 347 U.S. 483 (1954).

370 *See* Muller v. Oregon, 208 U.S. 412 (1908); *see also* Faigman, *Normative Constitutional Fact-Finding: Exploring the Empirical Component of Constitutional Interpretation*, *supra* note 160, at 566–573 (describing misuse of scientific evidence in these and other cases).

371 *See* Muller, 208 U.S. at 419.

372 *See id.*

opinion.[373] It served more to corroborate prevailing stereotypes than to provide a useful base of scientific knowledge.[374]

In *Brown v. Board of Education*, the Supreme Court ruled that segregating black school children violated the Fourteenth Amendment. Describing the effect of segregation on black school children, the court observed that school segregation "generates a feeling of inferiority as to their status in the community that may affect their hearts and minds in a way unlikely ever to be undone."[375] The court stated that its findings on the psychological impact of segregation are "amply supported by modern authority."[376] In a footnote that has been called "the most controversial . . . in American constitutional law,"[377] the Court then referenced a series of research studies.[378] Although no modern scholar would criticize the results in *Brown*, the studies and the implications drawn from those studies have been thoroughly trounced. One scholar describes in the following manner some of the criticisms of the Clark, Deutscher, and Chein studies cited in *Brown:*

> Perhaps the two most often cited criticisms of the Clarks' study are that: (1) Prof. Clark himself conducted the interviews with

---

373 John Monahan & Laurens Walker, Social Science in Law, 8 (3d Ed. 1994); *see also* James R.P. Ogloff, *Jingoism, Dogmatism and Other Evils, in* Psychology in the Courts: International Advances in Knowledge 1, 4 (Ronald Roesch et al. eds., 2001) (describing the extensive criticism of the Brandeis Brief across time).

374 Rebecca R. Zubaty, *Foreign Law and the U.S. Constitution: Delimiting the Range of Persuasive Authority*, 5 UCLA L. Rev. 1413, 1437 (2007) (describing problems in the use of inadequate empirical evidence in cases such as *Muller*).

375 *See* Brown v. Board of Ed., 347 U.S. 483, 494 (1954).

376 *See id.*

377 *See* Paul L. Rosen, *History and State of the Art of Applied Social Research in the Courts, in* The Use/Nonuse/Misuse of Applied Social Research 9 (Michael J. Saks & Charles H. Baron eds., 1980).

378 *See* Brown v. Board of Ed., 347 U.S. at 494 n. 11.

> the children who participated in the doll studies, a methodological flaw that can guide, if not bias, both responses and results; and, (2) the Clarks failed to indicate that northern Black children not subjected to segregation responded to the black and white dolls, in the main, in the same ways as segregated southern Black children. Deutscher and Chein were criticized for the biased nature of their survey sample—the vast majority of whom were liberal scientists studying race relations—that almost guaranteed that respondents would find segregation harmful.[379]

In addition to the *Brown* and *Muller* cases, the Supreme Court decisions related to jury size are cited as a particularly uncomfortable episode in the court's interactions with empirical evidence. In a pair of cases in the early 1970s, the Court found that reducing the size of juries from twelve members to six members in criminal and civil cases did not violate the constitutional right to a trial by jury.[380] In the later case, the Supreme Court cited "recent studies that provided convincing empirical evidence . . . that there is no discernible difference between the results reached by the two different-sized juries."[381] The Court's use of those studies has been sharply criticized on the grounds that the studies either did not support the proposition for which they were advanced, were not empirical studies, or were hopelessly flawed.[382]

---

379 Donald N. Bersoff, *The Not-so Weisman: The Supreme Court's Continuing Misuse of Social Science Research,* 2 U. CHI. L. SCH. ROUNDTABLE 279, 294 n.109 (1995).

380 *See* Colgrove v. Battin, 413 US 149 (1973); Williams v. Florida, 399 US 78 (1970).

381 *See* Colgrove, 413 U.S. at 159 n.15.

382 Bersoff, *supra* note 379, at 300–301; *see also* Michael J. Saks, *Ignorance of Science Is No Excuse*, 10 TRIAL 18 (Nov/Dec 1974); Hans Zeisel & Shari Seidman Diamond, *"Convincing Empirical Evidence" on the Six Member Jury*, 41 U. CHI. L. REV. 281 (1974).

Social scientists responded to these decisions by engaging in methodologically valid studies which found substantial differences between twelve-person and six-person juries. In the 1977 case of *Ballew v. Georgia*,[383] the Supreme Court then cited these later studies but in a distorted fashion. In announcing the judgment of the Court, Justice Blackman reaffirmed the six-person jury rule but cited the cases in support of the finding that a five-person jury would be insufficient. In other words, social science data, which found differences between six- and twelve-person juries, was ignored in reaffirming twelve-person juries. The same data, which had nothing to do with differences between five- and six-person juries, was then offered in declining to move from six to five people.[384] Those who would have preferred a more accurate use of social science data could perhaps take heart in the fact that only one of the other Justices signed onto the Blackmun opinion. Those who would have liked to see the Supreme Court use social science data more often, however, might have been less pleased with the concurring opinion signed by Justices Powell, Burger, and Rehnquist, which expressed reservations about the Blackmun opinion's "heavy reliance on numerology derived from statistical studies."[385] As one scholar noted, the dictionary definition of numerology is "a system of occultism built around numbers."[386]

In addition to misunderstanding scientific data, one might also worry about the numbing effects of reducing human

383 Ballew v. Georgia, 435 U.S. 223 (1977).

384 *See* Bersoff, *supra* note 379.

385 *See* Bellew, 433 U.S. 246 (Powell, J. concurring).

386 *See* Bersoff, *supra* note 379, at 301 & n.167 (noting that experimental psychologists heralded the Blackmun opinion as a resurgence of Supreme Court interest in social science, despite the fact that few justices signed on, but also noting that the Webster's dictionary definition of "numerology" is a system of occultism build around numbers.)

beings to data points. When we apply scientific analysis to social and behavioral issues, we may dehumanize the individuals who come through the legal system, creating the risk of engaging in morally troubling policies such as the eugenics decisions of the twentieth century.[387]

B. THE CHANGING NATURE OF LAW AND SCIENCE

The examples above describe concerns about whether legal actors understand the limitations of science and whether they can properly translate science into legal rules. In addition to an inaccurate understanding of science, however, law has an inaccurate vision of what science can do for us, given the nature of law. As described in Chapter V, law's evolutionary and adaptive processes break down when we try to import science into legal doctrine or export law's problems to science. It is the changing nature of law that makes science such a bad fit for legal doctrines.

This is not to suggest that science is unchanging or that nature, as the subject of science, is unchanging. Nature may evolve. More important, our ability to manipulate nature may evolve. Science is not merely about gaining an understanding of nature—seeking explanations to satisfy wonder.[388]

---

387 *See* ROSENBERG, *supra* note 219, at 8 (describing these concerns in the context of philosophy of science); *see also* Buck v. Bell, 274 U.S. 200, 207 (1927) (affirming forced sterilization of "mental defectives" on the grounds that "it is better for all the world, if instead of waiting to execute degenerate offspring for crime, or to let them starve for their imbecility, society can prevent those who are manifestly unfit from continuing their kind"); Paul Stephen Miller, *Genetic Testing & Disability Insurance,* 35 J.L. MED. & ETHICS 47, 48 (2007) (describing *Buck v. Bell*); Faigman, *Normative Constitutional Fact-Finding*, *supra* note 160, at 564 n.86 (same).

388 *See* ROSENBERG, *supra* note 216, at 22 (paraphrasing Aristotle).

Much of science is dedicated to manipulating nature, whether the subject is resisting cancer or resisting gravity. Although the enterprise of science assumes there are fundamental elements of the physical world that we try to understand, the purpose of our understanding may be to bend nature toward our will.

Thus, one could argue that the evolutionary character of law is not unique. Science changes and even nature, the topic of study in science, evolves itself. Nature may even evolve specifically to avoid our scientific efforts, although in limited circumstances. Bacteria, for example, can develop resistance to the medications we introduce, and cancer cells may find other pathways for growth as scientists block existing ones.

The question is not whether things in science change. The question is whether the way in which *law* changes makes science a bad fit for integration into legal doctrines. We follow the same failed paths again and again because we blind ourselves to the nature of legal evolution and to the limitations of what science can do for it.

Though the question is not whether law and science are similar because they both change, the question also is not whether science is different from law. It would be difficult to argue with the observation that science is different from law, at least on the level of a broad generalization. For example, if one asks whether law's questions are testable, in the sense that that they are capable of being tested, the answer would have to be no. As a society, we would never tolerate true experimentation in law. Law has an immediate responsibility to individuals, and it would be difficult to imagine judges saying, "lets convict this guy and see how well it works out." We think of the legal system as testing out theories, improving upon them and discarding those that work less well. The process may be evolutionary to some degree, in the sense that those things that work tend to remain and those that are clear failures tend to be discarded, but it is not experimental in the precise way that scientists would consider valid.

Legal academics can engage in some variants of experimentation or at least some forms of data analysis. They are working in the abstract, however, several layers removed from what can actually be tested, let alone what can be determined to have predictive capacity. They also must work with the unhappy constraint of having to deal with all those messy variables that cloud our ability to know whether the results we think we find are related to any reliable degree to our interpretation of them. It is a little like saying, "if you want to race a horse at maximum speed, first release its hand brake and pull away from the curb." One can make useful analogies between the law and science, but they are simply different beasts.

It isn't a matter of being inferior or superior. Such concepts make little sense when one is comparing things in different contexts. Champagne is inferior to rubbing alcohol in alcoholic content, for example, but that is unlikely to matter much on New Year's Eve.[389] Our failure to understand differences in the nature of law and science plays out in the unsuccessful choices we make as we reach for what we perceive to be superior.

Those who are more abstractly inclined also could compare science with law by asking whether law could ever exist outside of our perception of it. Science as an enterprise may be seriously flawed, but it presupposes the existence of an enduring nature that we can attempt to quantify and explain. There is an objective reality in nature, even if the human

---

389 *See* Machlup, *supra* note 303, at 151 (listing provocative comparisons of inferiority and superiority in the context of challenging whether social sciences are inferior to natural sciences).

perceiver is clouded in subjectivity. One could analogize to history as well. An event exists even if our ability to interpret it is affected by whether we have printing presses, TV video cameras, or webcams with desktop editing capabilities. Our ability to interpret the event will be further affected by the theories and philosophies that we bring to our interpretation. The existence of the event remains fixed, however, even if our understanding of the event may change across time.

One need not answer the metaphysical question of whether absolute concepts of law and justice exist outside of whatever structures we create or interpretations we impose, as interesting as that question may be. The problem is our desire for enduring structures in law and the consequences that result when we reach for what we perceive as enduring outside of law.

C. THE INCLUSION OF SOCIAL SCIENCE

Science is, almost by definition, what the layman cannot understand.

Fritz Machlup[390]

The prior chapters looked at specific examples of law's attempts to reach for science and the effects of those attempts. In looking at law's interactions with science, this book considers examples from the hard sciences, such as biology and physics, and from social sciences, such as economics and psychology. One could argue that only the hard sciences should be included, rather than any social sciences. If law is searching for certainty and reliability, the hard sciences would seem to offer stronger models to reach for than the social sciences.

---

390 Machlup, *supra* note 303, at 147.

Separating hard sciences from social sciences provides some of the same types of interesting puzzles as separating science from nonscience in general. Traditionally, the social sciences have included economics, psychology, sociology, anthropology, and political science.[391] The categories, nevertheless, are somewhat fluid. One philosopher, who would distinguish between the natural sciences and the social sciences on the basis of whether they are a generalizing science of nature or an individualizing historical science, would call economics a natural science and geology a historical one.[392] Others would include some subjects in the category of science that are normally regarded as social sciences or even humanities such as experimental psychology, linguistics, archeology, and economics.[393] As Kuhn noted, it is not a question of whether the natural sciences and the social sciences are different but rather how to draw the line between the two.[394]

In looking at law's attempts to reach for science, it is not surprising to see examples in which law treats social sciences like psychology and economics in ways quite similar to the way law treats the hard sciences. Among the social sciences, economics and psychology are considered the most mathematical and quantitative and therefore the most respectable from the point of view of similarity to the hard sciences.[395] Some would argue that despite the quantitative gloss, economics and psychology "do little more than dress up

---

391 Boston Studies, *supra* note 4, at 6.

392 *See* Machlup, *supra* note 303, at 136 (describing German Philosopher Heinrich Rickert who followed the philosopher Wilhelm Windelband).

393 *See also* Boston Studies, *supra* note 4, at 6.

394 *See* Thomas S. Kuhn, *The Natural and the Human Sciences*, *in* Klemke, *supra* note 49, at 129.

395 *See* Klemke, *supra* note 49, at 106.

well-known truths in jargon and numbers."[396] For my purposes, the question is not the nature or depth of revelation in these areas. Rather, the question is law's perception of these fields, particularly its perception of their authority and their majesty over concepts that we do not feel equipped to apply ourselves.

Problems emerge in law with things that we perceive of as "the authoritative other," something external to law that we interpret both as having superior reliability and as involving concepts that we cannot penetrate. Our perception of this "authoritative other" as having superior reliability allows us to indulge in the fantasy that it can rescue us from the discomfort of legal dilemmas and deliver the certainty that we crave. Our perception of this other as impenetrable makes us reluctant to fully engage with the concepts in a way that allows legal analysis to properly progress. As a result, our relationship to these external concepts is more hindrance than help in the unfolding of the legal process.

It is possible that examples lurk in our history in which law turns in the same way to other fields. Perhaps history and philosophy are also "others" to which we turn. The problems, however, are unlikely to be the same. Law's love affair with science leads us astray precisely because we feel incapable of engaging with science on an equal footing. We abdicate our responsibilities, reassuring ourselves that our problems are in the hands of something that is both superior and beyond our capabilities. We are far less likely to indulge in that abdication with fields that seem to be within our capabilities.

The social sciences, of course, have suffered from their own inferiority complex in relation to the natural sciences.

396 *See id.*

As Machlup noted, "social scientists, for some strange reason, are expected to foretell the future, and they feel badly if they fail."[397] Even the language we use to describe the fields harbors its own prejudices. We talk about "hard" science and "natural" science, words that connote more power and authority than "social" science. Bernard Cohen offers a wonderful riff on the subtle, pejorative implications of language and the difficulty of escaping from those implications. In comparing the natural sciences to the social sciences, he notes that the antonym for "natural" is "unnatural" and the antonym for "social" is "anti-social."[398] From that perspective, law would have to be both unnatural and anti-social.

Not to make too much of an academic's play on words, but the social sciences' experiences are instructive for the law. Law's efforts to emulate what we see as superior intellectual endeavors affect our vision of what counts as success and what counts as failure. It drives us toward behaviors that are counterproductive for the legal process.

---

397 *See* Machlup, *supra* note 303, at 147.

398 *See* Boston Studies, *supra* note 4, at xxvi.

CHAPTER VIII

Improving the Role of Science in Law

Although efforts to import science into law or to export law's problems to science may be misguided, science does have an important role to play in the legal process. As long as that role is properly recognized as supportive of rather than replacing the functioning of law, science can help guide and illuminate policy, while allowing the law to operate within its own parameters.

Despite the many times that the law has stumbled in its interactions with science, there are examples where the law has gotten it right. This chapter describes some of these examples, using them to help craft a more effective role for science in law. The chapter also suggests four approaches to help avoid our repeated pattern of failure: operating within law's parameters, using science for testing and transformation, protecting the structure of the dialogue, and embracing imperfection.

A. OPERATING WITHIN LAW'S PARAMETERS

Chapter III described law and economics arguments suggesting that law's domain should be circumscribed when the legal system cannot sufficiently engage in appropriate measurements.[399] The fallacy here is not that engaging in such measurements is problematic in a judicial setting but rather that measurement is always necessary. Science is dependent on measurement. Law is not. Even when law cannot measure something in an effective and efficient manner, law may still be able to use the insights of social science to craft legal doctrine.

Consider an example from the regulation of generic drugs. Regulators, consumers, scholars, Congress, and the president, among others have complained that patent holders and generic challengers are exploiting the regulatory system to enter into collusive settlements.[400] Critics argue that such

399 *See supra* notes 60–70 and accompanying text.

400 *See, e.g.*, FED. TRADE COMM'N, GENERIC DRUG ENTRY PRIOR TO PATENT EXPIRATION: AN FTC STUDY 10 (July 2002) ("[T]he provisions governing generic drug approval prior to patent expiration . . . are susceptible to strategies that, in some cases, may have prevented the availability of more generic drugs. These provisions continue to have the potential for abuse."); Saami Zain, *Sword or Shield? An Overview and Competitive Analysis of the Marketing of "Authorized Generics"*, 62 FOOD DRUG L.J. 739, 742 (2007) ("Recently, under the rubric of 'Lifecycle Management,' consultants and pharmaceutical executives have been encouraging various actions to squeeze the most profitability from existing drugs. Certain of these actions have been criticized as unethical, anticompetitive or even fraudulent." (footnotes omitted)); 148 CONG. REC. S7565, 7566 (daily ed. July 30, 2002) (statement of Sen. Hatch) (asserting that settlements between pharmaceutical companies and generic competitors that delay generic drug entry were an unanticipated outcome of the Hatch-Waxman Act); S. REP. NO. 107-67, at 4 (2002) ("Agreeing with smaller rivals to delay or limit competition is an abuse of the Hatch-Waxman law . . . ."); President George W. Bush, Remarks by the President on Prescription Drugs (Oct. 21, 2002) (criticizing pharmaceutical companies for undermining the regulatory scheme to keep generic

settlements keep all relevant generics off the market for a period of time and extend the time during which patent holders can charge inflated prices.[401] Without the benefit of competition from generic competitors, consumers pay higher drug prices, and the patent holder and generic company share the excess profits via the settlement payments.

The mechanism works by exploiting a provision in the Hatch-Waxman Act.[402] The Hatch-Waxman Act was intended, among other goals, to facilitate the entry of generic drugs into the market in the hopes of reducing the costs of medication.[403] The act tries to encourage generic companies to challenge invalid patents or patents that are being asserted against drugs to which they do not apply.[404] Toward this end,

---

drugs off the market), *available at* http://whitehouse.gov/news/releases/2002/10/print/20021021-2.html.

401 *See generally* C. Scott Hemphill, *Paying for Delay: Pharmaceutical Patent Settlement as a Regulatory Design Problem*, 81 N.Y.U.L. REV. 1553 (2006).

402 *See* 21 U.S.C. § 355(j)(2)(A)(vii) ("Hatch-Waxman Act") [Drug Price Competition and Patent Term Restoration Act of 1984 Pub. L. No. 98-417, 98 Stat. 1585 (1984) (codified as amended in 21 U.S.C. § 355, 35 U.S.C. § 156, 35 U.S.C. § 271 (e)(1) (2000)).]

403 *See id.;* Laba Karki, *Regulatory Amendments and Implications for Drug Patent Enforcement*, 87 J. PAT. & TRADEMARK OFF. SOC'Y, 602, 609 (2005) (describing the Hatch-Waxman Act); *see also* Abbott Labs. v. Young, 920 F.2d 984, 991 (D.C. Cir. 1990); *see also* H.R. REP. NO. 98-857, pt. I, at 14–15, 17 (1984). Among other provisions, the Act allows generic drug manufacturers to rely on safety and efficacy data provided by the original patent holder of the drug. *See* 21 U.S.C. § 355(j)(2)(A); *see also* Requirements for Submission of In Vivo Bioequivalence Data: Proposed Rule, 68 Fed. Reg. 61,640, 61,645 (Oct. 29, 2003) (reporting estimates of preparation and filing costs for generic drug applications between $300,000 and $1 million); Thomas Chen, Note, *Authorized Generics: A Prescription for Hatch-Waxman Reform*, 93 VA. L. REV. 459, 464 (2007).

404 Generic companies can challenge drug patents by asserting that either the "patent is invalid or will not be infringed by the manufacture, use, or sale of the new [generic] drug." 21 U.S.C. § 355(j)(2)(A)(vii)(IV). This is commonly called a "Paragraph IV certification."

the statute provides that the first generic drug company to file an application to market a generic equivalent of a patented drug will be granted 180 days of market exclusivity upon entering the market with their generic drug.[405] The Food and Drug Administration (FDA) will not allow other generics to enter the market until 180 days after the first generic company begins commercially marketing its generic drug. This provision gives generic companies an incentive to do battle against the big guns of major pharmaceutical companies.[406]

Some patent holders and generic companies have settled their disputes by entering into so-called reverse payment or pay-for-delay settlements.[407] In these settlements, the patent holder pays the generic challenger in exchange for the generic company's agreement to stay out of the market for a period of time. During that period of time, the Hatch-Waxman provisions operate to keep other generics from entering the market.[408] The generic company loses nothing

405 *See* 21 U.S.C. § 355(j)(5)(B)(iv). For detailed descriptions of this process, *see* Karki, *supra* note 400, at 609; Natalie M. Derzko, *The Impact of Recent Reforms of the Hatch-Waxman Scheme on Orange Book Strategic Behavior and Pharmaceutical Innovation,* 45 IDEA 165 (2005).

406 *See* Representative Henry Waxman, Speech at Generic Pharmaceutical Association's First Annual Policy Conference: Securing the Future of Affordable Medicine (Sept. 20, 2005) ("In exchange for undertaking the costs and risks of patent litigation, the successful challenger is given 6 months of marketing without any other generic competition."), *available at* http://www.house.gov/waxman/news_files/news_statements_generic_pharmaceutical%20_association_9.20.05.htm.

407 *See, e.g., in re* Buspirone Patent Litig., 185 F. Supp. 2d 363 (S.D.N.Y. 2002). They are called "reverse payments" because they involve payments from the plaintiff to the defendant—i.e. from the patentee to the generic manufacturer.

408 Ashlee B. Mehl, *The Hatch-Waxman Act and Market Exclusivity for Generic Drug Manufacturers: An Entitlement or an Incentive*, 81 CHI.-KENT L. REV. 649, 661 (2006); *see also* Press Release, Jon Leibowitz, FTC Commissioner,

because the 180-day market exclusivity period does not begin until the generic begins selling the product commercially.

With no competition in the market, the patent holder can keep the price of the drug at a high level, leaving plenty of profit to share with the generic company in the form of settlement payments. The potential for abuse in such cases is clear.[409] Nevertheless, settlements play an important role in the litigation process and embody judgments about the costs and risks of further litigation, regardless of the strength of the case.[410]

The difficult question, therefore, is whether and when to allow such payments. Here again, the problem of measurement rears its ugly head. For example, Carl Shapiro has suggested that such settlements should be evaluated in the

---

Concurring in Part and Dissenting in Part in the Matter of Cephalon, Inc., at 2, *available at* http://www.ftc.gov/os/caselist/0610182/080213comment.pdf. ("[T]he 180-day exclusivity, *which Congress created to reward generics for entering early*, does precisely the opposite: it extends the brand's monopoly, forcing consumers to pay excessive prices for [drugs] throughout the span of these illegal deals.").

409 *See, e.g.,* Mova Pharm. Corp. v. Shalala, 140 F.3d 1060, 1067 (D.C. Cir. 1998); *see also* Avery, *supra* note 11, at Part 5.2 ("The nature of patent monopolies creates an incentive for both parties in Paragraph IV infringement litigation to find a way to settle and split the monopoly profits.").

410 *See* Asahi Glass Co., Ltd. v. Pentech Pharms, Inc., 289 F. Supp. 2d 986, 994 (N.D. Ill. 2003) (Posner, J.) (noting that a ban on settlements in which the patentee explicitly pays the alleged infringer to stay out of the market would reduce the incentive to challenge patents by reducing the challenger's settlement options should he be sued for infringement, and so might well be thought anticompetitive); *see also* Thomas F. Cotter, *The Interface Between Intellectual Property Law and Antitrust Law: Commentary: Refining the "Presumptive Illegality" Approach to Settlements of Patent Disputes Involving Reverse Payments: A Commentary on Hovenkamp, Janis & Lemley*, 87 MINN. L. REV. 1789, 1809 (2003) (arguing that the danger of channeling Hatch-Waxman litigants toward settling away from settling on terms that involve reverse payments is that doing so threatens to reduce the value of pharmaceutical patents, including valid pharmaceutical patents).

following manner: The settlement should be permitted only if it would "generate at least as much surplus for consumers as they would have enjoyed had the settlement not been reached and the dispute instead resolved through litigation."[411] This is a wonderfully elegant solution to a complex problem. Unfortunately, it requires the type of complicated economic calculations that courts are simply incapable of applying.[412] How can a court hope to accurately measure consumer surplus, particularly the level of consumer surplus that would have existed in a hypothetical world where the parties had failed to settle?

We may be unable to measure the influence of a particular settlement on consumer surplus with any degree of precision. Nevertheless, our inability to measure should not prevent us from applying the insights of economics in crafting a solution. The solution to this problem lies not in asking the courts to measure but rather in asking the law to align the incentives of the parties with the incentives of society to the greatest extent possible.

For example, the Hatch-Waxman system provides many incentives for generics and patent holders to collude and

---

411 *See* Carl Shapiro, *Antitrust Limits to Patent Settlements*, 34 RAND J. ECON. 339, 393 (2003).

412 *Cf.* Daniel A. Crane, *Exit Payments in Settlement of Patent Infringement Lawsuits: Antitrust Rules and Economic Implications*, 54 FLA. L. REV. 747, 780 (2002) (arguing that "rather than attempting the likely impossible—and excessively costly—task of calculating the respective costs in every instance, courts . . . would do well to adopt presumptions about the relative costs of exit payment settlements based on the probability of the patentee's success on the merits"). For another approach to the problem, *see* Herbert Hovenkamp et al., *The Interface Between Intellectual Property Law and Antitrust Law: Anticompetitive Settlement of Intellectual Property Disputes*, 87 MINN. L. REV. 1719, 1720, 1760 n.179 (2003) (proposing that exclusion payments that exceed litigations costs should be presumptively illegal and rejecting approaches like Crane's that "require a more searching inquiry").

share the proceeds at little cost. The potential comes from the fact that both parties get a little surplus to share. That surplus comes from the potential to keep others, who are not party to the agreement, out of the market for the term of the settlement agreement. The parties thus can impose costs on third parties or consumers without having to take those costs into account.

Suppose, however, that we alter the 180-day exclusivity rules. Exclusivity might apply, for example, only if the generic challenger wins on the merits, not if the generic settles. If the two parties settle, other generics could still enter the market. Thus, the parties could not bargain in the shadow of the power to keep prices above a competitive level.[413] Indeed, the FDA originally read such a requirement (known, alternately, as the "successful defense" requirement or the "win-first" approach) into the Act.[414] The D.C. Circuit invalidated this requirement, however, holding that it violated the plain language of the Act.[415]

If we are concerned that such a rule would put too much pressure on avoiding settlement, other rules could be drafted. An alternative rule could be that the 180-day exclusivity period only applies if the challenger actually markets the drug. An agreement to postpone entry would void the exclusivity. Thus, a generic challenger could freely choose to settle. If it chooses to stay out of the market as part of the settlement, however, that decision comes at the cost of

---

413 *See* Marc L. Busch & Eric Reinhardt, *Bargaining in the Shadow of the Law: Early Settlement in GATT/WTO Disputes*, 24 FORDHAM INT'L L.J. 158 (2000).

414 *See* Mova Pharm. Corp. v. Shalala, 140 F.3d 1060, 1074 (D.C. Cir. 1998) (overturning an FDA requirement that the first generic challenger was only entitled to the 180-day exclusivity if it successfully defended against a patent infringement suit by the patent holder).

415 *See id.* at 1076.

allowing others generic competitors to enter. A second alternative rule could be to grant the exclusivity period only to the first *successful* generic challenger.[416] Under this scenario, if the first generic challenger settles, the exclusivity period would "roll-over" to the next challenger rather than being retained by the first challenger.[417] This type of "rolling exclusivity" would deter pay-for-delay settlements because it would be less feasible for patent holders to enter such settlements with all generic challengers.[418] Finally, if one is concerned that no other entrants are on the horizon, one could simply disallow settlements that pay challengers not to enter. Congress could choose one of these rules or leave the choice among such rules to courts or to the FTC, which has jurisdiction to challenge anticompetitive aspects of such settlements.[419]

In a similar vein, Daniel Crane suggested that a court should allow a patent holder to settle on such terms only if the patent holder is likely to win on the merits.[420]

---

416 Mehl, *supra* note 408, at 674. Recall that currently the 180-day exclusivity goes to the first generic applicant. Even if the first applicant fails to bring a generic equivalent to market, the 180-day exclusivity never rolls over to later applicants. *See* 21 U.S.C. § 355(j)(5)(D)(iii) (stating that if the first applicant withdraws, "no applicant shall be eligible" for the exclusivity period).

417 Mehl, *supra* note 408, at 674.

418 Avery, *supra* note 11, at Part 5.2.

419 For a detailed study of the proposed and the approved legislation, *see* Erika King Lietzan, *A Brief History of 180-Day Exclusivity Under the Hatch-Waxman Amendments to the Federal Food, Drug, and Cosmetic Act*, 59 FOOD & DRUG L.J. 287, 309–14 (2004).

420 *See* Crane, *supra* note 412, at 782 ("In general, however, the costs of prohibiting exit payments increase as the probability of the patentee's success increases, and the costs of permitting exit payments generally decrease as the probability of the patentee's success decreases. At high levels of probability that the patentee will prevail in the lawsuit, the costs of prohibiting exit payments outweigh the costs of permitting them, and vice versa.

The argument is that if the patent holder succeeds, the generic will be barred from the market for infringement.[421] Under those circumstances, the patent holder could choose to bargain away some of the power to exclude the generic in exchange for avoiding the cost of litigation.

This approach requires that a court evaluate the merits of the case from the perspective of the patent holder's likelihood of success.[422] Evaluating the likelihood of legal success is something courts are far better equipped to handle than measuring consumer surplus.[423] In fact, courts engage in precisely this inquiry to rule on a request for a preliminary injunction.[424] Once again, solutions exist if we focus on the types of tasks that the legal system is designed to accomplish.

Exit payments should therefore be permitted when the probability that the patentee will succeed is high, and be disallowed when the probability that the patentee will succeed is low.").

421 *See id.*

422 *See* Crane, *supra,* note 412, at 780 ("The higher the likelihood that the patentee's infringement claim is valid, the more likely it is that the costs of a rule prohibiting exit settlement payments outweigh the costs of permitting the exit payment, and vice versa. Thus, making some ex ante judgment about the merits of the infringement lawsuit is necessary to determine whether the exit payment should be permitted or prohibited.").

423 Crane's test becomes far more complex as the author suggests a follow up four-part inquiry, including an evaluation of whether the settlement payments reflect a large proportion of patentee's rents from patent disallowed. *See* Crane, *supra* note 412, at 783–96. Nevertheless, the test could be crafted as the more streamlined "likelihood of success on the merits" inquiry.

424 *See, e.g.,* Pfizer, Inc. v. Teva Pharm., USA, Inc., 429 F.3d 1364, 1372 (Fed. Cir. 2005) (noting in a patent infringement case that for a preliminary injunction to issue, a court must consider whether the patent owner has shown: (a) a reasonable likelihood of success on the merits; (b) the prospect of irreparable harm to the patent owner in the absence of the injunction; (c) that this harm would exceed harm to the alleged infringer when subject to the injunction; and (d) that granting the injunction is in the public interest).

Congress eventually chose a combination of the rules outlined above. In 2003, Congress amended the Hatch-Waxman Act so that the generic first-filer will forfeit its exclusivity if it does not market the drug within a specified period of receiving FDA approval to market its generic equivalent.[425] This "failure to market" forfeiture provision was intended to deter pay-for-delay settlements by removing the ability of the patent holders to bottleneck generic competition by entering into an agreement with the first generic challenger.[426]

The 2003 Amendments also contain more expansive language in recognition of the fact that companies may be quite creative in their efforts to collude. Specifically, the Amendments provide that the generic first-filer forfeits exclusivity it if enters into any agreement that "violate[s] the antitrust laws."[427] This, again, reduces the incentive for generics and patent holders to collude by creating a remedy that can be used by courts and antitrust agencies in the form of a flexible standard.[428]

---

425 *See* 21 U.S.C. § 355(j)(5)(D)(i)(I) (2005); *see also* Medicare Prescription Drugs, Improvement, and Modernization Act of 2003, Pub. L. No. 108-173, 117 Stat. 2066 (effective Dec. 8, 2003); Mehl, *supra* note 405 at 668–70; Avery, *supra* note 11, at Part 4.3.

426 *See* 149 Cong. Rec. S15746 (2003) (Senator Schumer stated that the revisions were designed to ensure that the 180-day exclusivity period "cannot be used as a bottleneck" to generic drug entry).

427 *See* 21 U.S.C. § 355(j)(5)(D)(i)(V).

428 Unfortunately, the revised Act raised a host of new interpretative questions that pharmaceutical companies have successfully manipulated to keep generic drugs off the market. The FDA has interpreted the revised Hatch-Waxman Act so that the 180-day exclusivity period is almost never forfeited, even when the generic company enters into a reverse payment settlement with the pharmaceutical patent holder. *See* Avery, *supra* note 11, at Part 5.2.

Congress' final choice among the rules is less important than the fact that such potential rules exist. Many of the rules described above would alter the settlement incentives among the parties. We have no need to measure the consumer surplus that the parties might be exploiting to address their ability to engage in such exploitation. Nor do we need to ignore the economic insights that demonstrate the potential for such exploitation. Rather, we can take those insights and craft rules to address a potential problem without extensive measurement and within the parameters of law.

I am not suggesting that all measurement should be excised from legal tests. Nor can I claim that all legal tests can be crafted by aligning incentives. The point is that the more we can stick to rules that reflect the types of tasks the law is designed to accomplish, the better results we will have. This is particularly true when we are trying to benefit from the insights of science, a process that can easily lead law astray.

From a very broad perspective, therefore, I agree with Judge Easterbrook's suggestion that we try to establish presumptions and screening rules that can minimize the amount of measurement in which a court must engage.[429] The problem occurs, however, when the scales are tipped—for example, when measurement is accepted only for inquiries that lead to one type of result and not for inquiries that would lead in another direction.[430] In short, science works best, not when law defers to science, but rather when we use scientific insights to help craft legal rules within the proper parameters of a legal inquiry.

---

429 *See supra* text accompanying notes 62–69 (discussing Judge Easterbrook's antitrust proposals).

430 *See supra* text accompanying notes 65–66 (discussing problems with Judge Easterbrook's proposals).

The same type of approach can be used to formulate rules for patenting genetic inventions. Rather than fixating on a single, scientific line such as nucleoside sequence, courts should delve into the more substantive legal analysis, which would ask, "what was the problem to be overcome, what was the advancement created, and was the advancement a significant leap from what was available in the field?" This is the type of inquiry contemplated in American patent law and applied in genetic patent cases in other legal systems.[431] Science can provide insights helpful to this analysis, but those insights should not be transformed into doctrinal rules.

B. TESTING AND TRANSFORMATION

Although legal rules drawn by reference to scientific lines are not well suited to the process of interpretation, evolution, and adaptation that is essential to the enterprise of law, science can help evaluate the assumptions underlying the legal rules courts develop. As David Faigman explained,

431 For example, the European patent system requires inventors to demonstrate an "inventive step" in order to secure a patent. European Patent Convention, Article 52 ("European patents shall be granted for any inventions . . . provided that they are new, involve an inventive step and are susceptible of industrial application."). *See also* Bradford L. Smith & Susan O. Mann, *Innovation and Intellectual Property Protection in the Software Industry: An Emerging Role for Patents?*, 71 U. CHI. L. REV. 241, 271 (2004) (noting the European system requires an "inventive step" over prior art for patentability; *cf.* Shayana Kadidal, *Subject-Matter Imperialism? Biodiversity, Foreign Prior Art and The Neem Patent Controversy* 37 IDEA 371, 389 n.94 (discussing the German patent system's allowance of "petty patents" for inventions demonstrating an "incremental" improvement on existing state of the art). *See also* NATIONAL ACADEMIES, *supra* note 7, at 93 (criticizing the American doctrine and noting that all other industrialized countries approach the nonobviousness of novel genes by focusing on the technical hurdles faced by the inventor.).

science restrains courts by making them accountable for the normative judgments underlying their factual suppositions.[432] "Brute reality restrains the Court."[433]

The revelations of science can be used to encourage courts to reevaluate decisions resting on shaky foundations. A successful example of this approach can be seen in the area of civil commitment laws. In *Parham v. J.R.*, the Supreme Court considered what process is required when parents voluntarily commit their children to state mental hospitals.[434] The Court ruled that Constitutional due process requires that the child be evaluated by a neutral fact finder, such as a mental health professional who has the authority to refuse to admit the child to the hospital if the child does not satisfy the proper medical standards. Nevertheless, due process does not require judicial review of the decision.[435]

The Court supported its ruling, in part, with the judgment that "the state through its involuntary commitment procedures does not 'label' the child."[436] Subsequent research suggests that children are indeed labeled and stigmatized by such commitments.[437] This research casts doubt on the validity of the Court's legal conclusions and has been the basis of criticism of the decision.[438]

---

432 *See* David L. Faigman, *"Normative Constitutional Fact-Finding": Exploring the Empirical Component of Constitutional Interpretation,* 139 U. PA. L. REV. 541, 548 (1991) (discussing science in the context of Supreme Court jurisprudence) (hereinafter *Normative Constitutional Fact-Finding*).

433 *See id.*

434 *See* Parham v. J.R., 442 U.S. 584, 606 (1979).

435 *See id.* at 606–07.

436 *See id.* at 600–01.

437 *See* Melton, *Family and Mental Hospital as Myths: Civil Commitment of Minors, in* CHILDREN, MENTAL HEALTH, AND THE LAW 151, 158–59 (N. Reppucci, L. Weithorn, E. Mulvey & J. Monahan eds. 1984).

438 *See, e.g.,* Faigman, *Normative Constitutional Fact-Finding, supra* note 160, at 586.

In a similar vein, the revelations of science can certainly transform law, although not replace it. The dramatic effect of DNA evidence on doctrines related to paternity provides a good example. Prior to the development of DNA testing, state laws contained a series of presumptions to address the question of paternity. DNA evidence in theory would eliminate the need for such presumptions, providing a simple method for settling the question of biological fatherhood. No scientific test, however, could resolve the many questions surrounding the legal notion of parenthood and the resulting rights and responsibilities.

If paternity were simply a matter of DNA, one would expect that a man who has been supporting a child and discovers he is not the father of the child would be relieved of any financial burden. Such is not necessarily the case. Courts will consider the broad range of the father's behavior and the best interests of the child in determining whether such support must continue.

For example, in the recent case of *S.R.D. v. T.L.B.*,[439] a man and woman were married for nine years, during which time the wife gave birth to three children. In the divorce petition, the man stated that he was the father of all three children and agreed to joint custody and child support.[440] Six years after the divorce, paternity tests revealed that the youngest could not possibly be his daughter.[441] Returning to court, the man asked to be relieved of financial support obligations for the youngest but argued that as the only father the child had ever known, he should continue to have visitation rights and a parental relationship with her.[442]

---

439 *See* S.R.D. v. T.L.B., 174 S.W. 3d. 502 (2005).

440 *See id.* at 503.

441 *See id.*

442 *See id.* at 504.

In denying the man's petition, the court noted that although from a purely genetic standpoint, the man was not the father, there was no doubt that a man can be a legal father without being a biological one.[443] Having held himself out as the girl's father for an extended period of time, despite possible doubts along the way, the court concluded that the man could not now disavow the relationship. "The relationship of father and child is too sacred to be thrown off like an old cloak, used and unwanted. . . . The law is not so insensitive as to countenance the breach of an obligation in so vital and deep a relation, undertaken, partially fulfilled, and suddenly sundered."[444]

Other courts similarly have applied equitable doctrines to prevent men from withdrawing financial support from non-biological children.[445] Despite the scientific evidence, the absence of a biological link can be outweighed by the interest of the child, the interests of the mother, the interests of society, or even the interests of other children in the family.[446]

Thus, in the case of DNA paternity evidence, scientific information did influence legal doctrine, altering the series

443 *See id.* at 508.

444 *See id.* at 510–511.

445 *See, e.g.,* Hubbard v. Hubbard 44 P.3d 153 (Alaska 2002) (finding that stepfather who had never completed adoption of stepchild but had "made his heart and soul available to the child" and encouraged the mother to relinquish support from the biological father could not disavow those obligations after separating from the mother); Betty L.W. v. William E.W., 212 W.VA. 1 (W.Va. 2002) (holding that paternity test taken 5 years after divorce proceeding would not be admitted to reopen support obligations).

446 *See* cases cited *supra* note 442; S.R.D. v. T.L.B., 174 S.W. 3d. at 503 (upholding family court finding that the family court concluded that any financial or emotional disruption of the parent-child relationship with the youngest child would be seriously detrimental to all three children).

of presumptions embedded in the law.[447] The scientific information, however, resolved only part of the legal dilemmas and could not replace the complex analysis that determines a child's paternity.

In short, while science cannot tell us how to craft an appropriate legal rule, science can play an important role in testing the assumptions underlying legal rules as the legal system develops those rules. This evaluative role integrates well with law's natural process of interpretation and adaptation. Science thereby operates within law's domain but consistent with the parameters of the legal process.

C. PROTECTING THE STRUCTURE OF THE DIALOGUE

> *[W]e can only convince an interlocutor if at some point he shares our understanding of the language concerned. If he does not, there is no further step to take in rational argument.*
>
> Charles Taylor[448]

As described in Chapter V, law is constantly driven to adapt to changing circumstances through various spheres of acceptance. This process of Bounded Adaptation cannot proceed effectively without an adequately structured dialogue

447 *See, e.g.*, Department of Human Services v. Chisum, 85 P.3d 860, 861–62 (Okla. Ct. App. 2004) (stating that genetic testing could establish a mistake of material fact that would satisfy the elements for disestablishment of paternity if brought in a timely fashion); Cal. Fam. Code § 7646(a)(1) (establishing a 2-year period for genetic disestablishment).

448 Charles Taylor, *Interpretation and the Sciences of Man*, *in* KLEMKE, *supra* note 49, at 112–13 (comparing the Hegelian rationalist approach and the empiracist approach to "breaking out" from the "circle of illusion" comprising the individual's own isolated intuitive perspective and the consequent inability to see other perspectives).

that will promote the flow of information and analysis. Where law and science must interact, two elements are critical for protecting this dialogue: speaking a common language and avoiding insularity.

First, if scientific insights are going to play a supportive role in the legal process, they must be expressed in a language that legal actors can understand. Parroting technical language can obscure an inability to grasp the full meaning and implications of an issue. It creates the temptation to engage in a form of sophistry, to speak in what Nussbaum describes, in the context of philosophy, as a seductive, jargon-filled way that leads us to believe we have mastered something deep for having learned to use the jargon.[449] We cannot effectively engage in the process of interpretation and adaptation unless we are speaking a common language.

Jargon also is the perfect vehicle for strategic behavior. It allows legal actors to use broad open-ended language and then argue later that whatever position they wish surely falls within the language chosen.[450] As one international patent examiner noted in frustration:

> In these claims, the numerous variables and their voluminous, complex meanings and their seemingly endless permutations, makes it virtually impossible to determine the full scope and

---

449 *See* Nussbaum, *supra* note 13, at 1641; *see also* ROBERT K. MERTON & NORMAN W. STORER, THE SOCIOLOGY OF SCIENCE 264 (noting that esoteric scientific terminology separates the laity from understanding and the "population at large has become ripe for new mysticisms clothed in apparently scientific jargon").

450 *See* Feldman, *Inventor's Contribution*, *supra* note 43, at text accompanying note 24 (noting that the emergence of the separate written description doctrine reflected concerns about patent holders who mark out broad territory with their claims and then fill in information later, either as their own research advances or as they see the research of others advance).

> complete meaning of the claimed subject matter . . . it is impossible to carry out a meaningful search on same.[451]

Given the challenges of effective dialogue at the law and science interface, law should move toward describing scientific and technological issues in plain language, wherever possible. Even in patent drafting, which embodies some of the most challenging aspects of translation in the law and science interface, a move toward plain language would be a significant improvement. If legal actors cannot understand the full implications of the terms being used, they cannot do an adequate job of considering the legal questions surrounding the precedents. They are, in essence, flying blind.

In explaining this proposal, it is important to note that most legal actors have no scientific expertise. District court judges charged with patent interpretation are unlikely to have any scientific expertise. The same is true for the jurors, who must decide other elements of patent cases. Even the specialized judges of the Federal Circuit may have little knowledge or experience relevant to a particular case. Most Federal Circuit judges have neither a technical background nor patent experience when they are appointed to the bench.[452] For those who do have some scientific training, their training may have occurred decades before, an eternity away from modern computer and genetic technologies.

---

451 *See* Derek Lowe, *The Examiner Finally Snaps*, Corante (January 24, 2006), available at http://www.corante.com/pipeline/archives/2006/01/24/the_examiner_finally_snaps.php (quoting a patent examiner who was charged with writing a search report on a patent application for the nations that belong to the Patent Cooperation Treaty).

452 *See* Kimberly A. Moore, 15 HARV. J. LAW & TECH. 1, 18 (2001) (noting that only "four of the twelve active Federal Circuit judges have technical backgrounds").

Finally, whatever training a judge may have will relate to certain areas of patent law but not to others. As one commentator noted, "[a] patent litigation relating to a modern chipset bears little resemblance to a case where the invention at issue is the derivation of a yeast species for the production of a recombinant protein nutritional supplement that makes farm-raised salmon pink."[453] For those without a science background, it is easy to assume that training and expertise in one scientific field confers wisdom in all scientific fields. Other than perhaps creating a lack of fear, however, knowledge in one scientific area does not necessarily translate into knowledge in another.

Some judges are remarkably skilled at translating scientific lingo into concepts that can be molded into legal doctrine.[454] For most legal actors, however, the challenge of penetrating scientific jargon creates a tendency to defer to scientists and to avoid delving deeply into the essence of the case.

The problem is not just that patents are written using scientific language, patents also are written in the form of an arcane code. Claims are written in a single sentence, making the language tremendously convoluted.[455] In addition, words have particularized meanings that will be understood only by the properly initiated.

For example, patent applicants must describe the best mode of making their invention.[456] In describing that mode,

---

453 Sung, *supra* note 504, at 28–29.

454 *See, e.g.,* SmithKline Beecham Corp. v. Apotex Corp., 247 F. Supp. 2d 1011 (N.D.Ill.2003) (Posner, J. sitting by designation).

455 *See* Ana Cristina Almeida Muller, Nei Pereina Jr., & Adelaide Maria de Souza Antunes, *Protecting Biotechnological Inventions in Brazil and Abroad: Draft, Scope, and Interpretation of Claims*, 13 ALB. L.J. SCI & TECH. 145, 158.

456 *See* 35 U.S.C. § 112 (2005).

applicants may explain a manner and process of making the invention that they have not actually engaged in but that they believe is the best mode.[457] The code for signaling the difference between work that an inventor has actually engaged in and work that an inventor has not, involves verb tense.[458] Subtle verb changes are unlikely to mean much to the uninitiated, regardless of whether that person has a science degree. It would be so much clearer and simpler if the patent applicant said, "This is an example of what we believe the best mode of making the invention should be, although we have not yet performed each step in this precise order."

Patent law's word interpretation can be downright incomprehensible under common sense notions of language. For example, in the recent case of *Baldwin v. Siebert*,[459] the Federal Circuit interpreted the phrase "a pre-soaked fabric role." In overturning the lower court's interpretation of the word, the Federal Circuit explained that the indefinite article "a" can mean "more than one" unless the patent holder evidences a clear intent to limit the meaning of the word.[460] The court noted the following: "that 'a' or 'an' can mean 'one or more' is best described as a rule, rather than as a presumption or even a convention."[461]

---

457 *See* Manual of Patent Examining Procedure § 608.01(p) (8th ed., 2001). Work that an inventor has not done yet is known as a paper example. *See* Hoffman La Roche Inc. v. Promega Corp., 323 F.3d 1354, 1375 n.2 (Fed. Cir. 2003) (Newmann, J. dissenting).

458 *See* Hoffman La Roche v. Promega, 323 F.3d at 1354 (invalidating a patent for using the words "the results show," which was ruled to be past tense when present tense was required).

459 Baldwin Graphic Systems, Inc. v. Siebert, Inc., 512 F.3d. 1338 (Fed. Cir. 2008).

460 *See id.* at 1342.

461 *See id.*

Patent law is full of such code-like communication. For example, suppose a patent holder describes an invention as comprising x, y, and z components. Now, one might think that the invention is made up only of x, y, and z. Not so. "Comprising" is in an open-ended code word representing the fact that the invention could include elements not actually listed.[462] The word "consisting" is the proper code word used to indicate that the elements listed are the only elements.[463]

Rather than trying to parse the difference between an invention "comprised of" something and an invention "consisting of" something, one could simply use plain language to explain that the components "include but are not limited to the following." A plain language description not only communicates more clearly to those who must interpret the patent, it also increases the pressure on patent holders to actually define what they are trying to claim, rather than leaving the claim open-ended with the intention of filling in the gaps as other products emerge on the market.[464]

Most important, plain language allows judges to more easily understand the implications of their decisions and puts pressure on judges to take responsibility for those decisions. In particular, for judges who *do* have technical expertise, a plain language system avoids the temptation to suggest "we, in the club know it when we see it, and that is good

---

462 *See* Shanshan Zhang, *Proposing Resolutions to the Insufficient Gene Patent System,* 20 SANTA CLARA COMPUTER & HIGH TECH. L.J. 1139, 1157–58 & n.147 (2004); Gillette Co. v. Energizer Holdings, Inc., 405 F.3d 1367, 1371 (Fed. Cir. 2005) (noting that using the word comprising in a patent is a "signal" that the list if items in the group is open-ended).

463 *See id.; see also* Jorge A. Goldstein & Elina Golod, Human Gene Patents, 77 Acad. Med. 1315, 1319 (Dec. 2002).

464 *See* Zhang, *supra* note 459, at 1158.

enough." The requirement for clear and plain communication keeps legal actors faithful to supportable logic rather than subject to the whims of prejudice masked in obscurity.

It is ironic that in our efforts to increase the status of the legal system we risk creating the opposite effect. As one scholar has noted in the social science world, using ordinary words with specialized meanings has a tendency to evoke contempt. Those outside the specialized field frequently respond with anger or condescending amusement.[465] Yet the legal system is using such specialized meanings in a forum that can never contain only relevant specialists. To the extent that the coded language flows from patent law, it risks drawing the contempt of inventors who see the system as strangely distorted. To the extent the coded language flows from scientific usage, it risks drawing the contempt of the nonscientists who must ponder the cases, including judges, law clerks, and jurors, not to mention members of Congress and the popular press. Thus, the specialized code language of the patent law system may be ineffective not only as an approach to a properly functioning legal system but also as a method of enhancing law's image.

The legal system already has a good model for requiring that participants draft in plain language. Since 1998, the Securities and Exchange Commission (SEC) has required companies to draft key sections of their disclosure documents in plain language.[466] The program has turned ponderous, impenetrable documents into more understandable

465 *See* Machlup, *supra* note 303, at 148.

466 *See* Michael G. Byers, *Eschew Obfuscation—the Merits of the SEC's Plain English Doctrine,* 31 U. Mem. L. Rev. 135, 137 (2000); *see also* 17 C.F.R. § 230.421(d) (2000).

communications.[467] The same spirit, although perhaps not precisely the same approach, could be applied to patents.

As with the SEC's program, implementing a plain language standard for patents might be possible with regulatory action rather than legislative action. The Patent and Trademark Office (PTO) has authority to govern the conduct of proceedings before its office, including the proper form of a patent application and requirements for additional information.[468] The Federal Circuit already has interpreted this authority broadly, finding that it includes the right to demand a zone of information beyond what is material to patentability and beyond what is directly useful for supporting a rejection or conclusively deciding the issue of patentability.[469]

The penalty for failure to comply with plain language requirements need not be draconian. It would be unfortunate

---

467 For discussion of the SEC plain language program, *see* Byers, *supra* note 463; Andrew T. Serafin, *Kicking the Legalese Habit: The SEC's "Plain English Disclosure" Proposal,* 29 Loyola U. Chi. L.J. 681 (1998); *see also* Securities and Exchange Commission, A Plain English Handbook: How to Create Clear SEC Disclosure Documents, *available at* http://www.sec.gov/pdf/handbook.pdf [hereinafter SEC Handbook]; Steven L. Schooner, *Communicating Governance: Will Plain English Drafting Improve Regulation?,* 70 Geo. Wash L. Rev. 163 (2002).

For example, the phrase "no consideration or surrender of Beco Stock will be required of shareholders of Beco in return for the shares of Unis Common Stock issued pursuant to the Distribution" becomes the following: "You will not have to turn in your shares of Beco stock or pay any money to receive your shares of Unis common stock from the spinoff." *See* SEC Handbook, *supra* at 464.

468 *See* 35 U.S.C. § 2(b)(2) (2000) (formerly at 35 U.S.C. § 6(a) (1988)).

469 *See* Star Fruits v. U.S., 393 F.3d 1277, 1282 (Fed. Cir. 2005). In addition, the Federal Circuit has expressed approval of PTO regulations that encourage examiners to use the power granted by Congress to perform the best quality examination possible. *See id.* One can easily argue that requiring patent information to be drafted in plain language terms that more clearly communicate the contours of the invention enhances the PTO's ability to perform a quality examination.

if such requirements became an additional weapon in the arsenal of aggressive litigators trying to overturn a patent. Rather, the PTO could enforce the plain language requirement by requesting that patent holders rewrite jargon-laden applications as part of the back-and-forth requests for information during the patent examination process or by denying expedited review for those who refuse to comply.[470]

With SEC disclosure documents, the goal is to translate words that reflect financial transactions and embody limitations on legal liability into language that a person with no legal or financial training can understand. With plain language patents, the goal is to translate scientific jargon into language that a legal actor with little or no scientific background can understand.

Clarifying science is certainly a challenge, but the process of translation from one field to the next is a challenge fields other than science face. As Nussbaum has noted in reference to philosophy, philosophy is sometimes written in a fussy and jargon-laden way, leading people to think that it has nothing to offer the person immersed in life.[471] Nevertheless, the history of medical ethics in the United States shows that philosophers are perfectly capable of learning what they need to learn to speak to professionals in other disciplines.[472]

---

470 *See* Accelerated Patent Examination, United States Patent and Trademark Office (Sept. 20, 2007), *available at* http://www1.uspto.gov/go/com/strat21/action/aep10.htm (discussing the requirements for accelerated examination under the current regulatory schema); *cf.* Staff Legal Bulletin No. 7 (Sept. 4, 1998), *available at* http://www.sec.gov/interps/legal/slbcf7.htm; Byers, *supra* note 463, at 170 (noting the SEC penalty for refusal to comply with plain language regulations is the right to deny acceleration of the effective dates of registration statements).

471 *See* Nussbaum, *supra* note 13, at 1641–42.

472 *See id.*

Before I am burned at the stake for heresy, I should explain the limitations of what I suggest. Plain language patents will not, by any stretch of the imagination, solve all of the problems in patent interpretation.[473] Language will always be subject to varying interpretations, no matter how clear and plain one tries to make it. Moreover, patents by their very nature describe something innovative. Many patent holders find themselves in the difficult position of trying to use existing language to describe something that didn't exist when the language developed.[474]

---

473 *See, e.g.,* Phillips v. AWH Corp., 415 F.3d 1303, 1314 (Fed. Cir. 2005) (en banc), *cert. denied*, 126 S.Ct. 1332 (2006) (describing the many possible sources to consider for interpreting claim language and noting that the meaning of a claim term as understood by persons of skill in the art is often not immediately apparent). For recent discussions of the problems in claim construction, *see* Andrew S. Brown, *Amgen v. HMR: A Case for Deference in Claim Construction*, 21 HARV. J.L. & TECH. 479 (2007); Christopher A. Cotropia, *Patent Claim Interpretation Methodologies and Their Claim Scope Paradigms*, WM. & MARY L. REV. 49 (2005); Andrew B. Dzeguze, *Did Markman and Phillips Answer the Right Question? A Review of the Fractured State of Claim Construction Law and the Potential Use of Equity to Unify It*, 15 TEX. INTELL. PROP. L.J. 457 (2007); Jeffrey A. Lefstin, *Claim Construction, Appeal, and the Predictability of Interpretive Regimes*, 61 U. MIAMI L. REV. 1033 (2007); Kelly Casey Mullally, *Patent Hermeneutics: Form and Substance in Claim Construction*, 59 FLA. L. REV. 333 (2007); Kristen Osenga, Linguistics & Patent Claim Construction, 38 RUTGERS L.J. 61 (2006); Ehab M. Samuel, Phillips v. AWH Corp., Inc.: A Baffling Claim Construction Methodology; 16 FORDHAM INTELL. PROP. MEDIA & ENT. L.J. 519 (2006); David Sanker, Phillips v. AWH Corp.: No Miracles in Claim Construction, 21 BERKELEY TECH. L.J. 101 (2006); Michael Saunders, A Survey of Post-Phillips Claims Construction Cases, 22 BERKELEY TECH. L.J. 215 (2007).

474 *See* Radin, *supra* note 201, at 6; *see also* Bridgeford, 357 F.2d at 682 (arguing that "[T]he right to a patent on an invention is not to be denied because of the limitations of the English language. . . . [T]he limitations of known technology concerning the subject matter sought to be patented should not arbitrarily defeat the right to a patent on an invention").

It is also true that an invention described in a patent frequently must be compared to products that did not exist at the time of the patent. This makes patent drafting a particularly challenging enterprise, which could suggest that we should give drafters some leeway to speak in strange tongues. Applying precedent to circumstances that did not exist at the time the precedent developed, however, is the essence of interpretation throughout the legal system.[475] Patents are no different from other precedents such as cases, codes, and constitutions.[476] In short, patent law, like any other area of law, is essentially a process of legal interpretation, which must be carried out in the common language of such interpretation.

Some would suggest that such an enterprise is doomed from the start. Philosophers such as Lakoff and Winter argue that there are no concepts or categories that humans share on an innate level but only metaphors built through social consensus. These things do not exist on an abstract level but are formed by our experiences and by the words chosen to describe those experiences.[477] Words are "metaphorical mappings" that actually create our understanding of something, rather than merely identifying it.[478] This is true for abstractions such as justice as well as concrete categories such as food.

---

475 *See supra* text accompanying notes 196–207.

476 *See infra* p.1 (comparing patent interpretation to Constitutional interpretation).

477 For an extensive description of Lakoff, Winter, and the concepts described in this section, *see* James E. Penner, *Cognitive Science, Legal Theory, and the Possibility of an Observation/Theory Distinction in Morality and Law, in* Reece, *supra* note 53.

478 *See* Penner, *supra* note 474, at 11–13 (describing Lakoff and arguing that law is transformative as choices of legal metaphors alter the way legal doctrine develops).

From this perspective, the notion of speaking in a common language makes little sense. There are no concepts generally shared and therefore no commonly shared language. In particular, the experiences of scientists and lawyers vary so greatly that no common language would be possible.

This notion, which I call conceptual indeterminacy, has been sharply criticized. A favorite example of mine is Penner's response to Lakoff's analysis of lust. Lakoff argues that the concept of lust exists only as a construct of the metaphors we use to describe it, including animal heat, insanity, and automobile motors. Lust does not exist in some abstract, independent manner. Rather, the linguistic devices chosen to describe it and the experiences from which we choose those devices form its identity.

Penner is doubtful that concepts are so dependent on experience and linguistic devices for their existence. After all, says Penner, he and the !Kung tribesmen would both be able to realize that Fred over there is behaving in a lustful fashion to Beatrice, even though the tribesmen have never seen an automobile.[479] Thus, they will be able to understand each other's concept of lust, even if the metaphors used to describe those concepts arise from experiences that cannot be shared. Although fairly basic, the tribesmen example helps to bring home the notion that concepts can exist in an independent, enduring fashion outside of our language or experience. As Fodor explains, "the concept isn't coming from the environment, it's coming from the organism."[480]

Most important, to the extent that experiences do differ, we need to be particularly wary of using language and

479 *See* Penner, *supra* note 477, at 22–23.

480 FODOR, REPRESENTATIONS: PHILOSOPHICAL ESSAYS ON THE FOUNDATIONS OF COGNITIVE SCIENCE 280 (1981) (explaining this concept in the context of the way children learn language).

metaphors that will be untranslatable outside of whatever common ground exists. Scientific jargon ensures lack of translation in a legal setting. Some who argue for conceptual indeterminacy extend this notion to argue that the language chosen in law is itself transformative. Different metaphors brought into case opinion alter the understanding of the legal doctrine itself and the view of behavior that should or should not be tolerated.[481]

Although legal metaphor can be tremendously powerful, it does have limits. If law could transform by metaphor, the public by now should be able to accept unauthorized music downloading as "theft." Nevertheless, only a few persistent folks, such as those whose parents are law professors, actually behave in a manner that manifests equating music downloading with stealing from a department store.

Similarly, as Penner notes, some legal metaphors fail because they are simply counter to our innate understanding of the concepts. For example, attempts to characterize rape as just another form of theft failed because they run counter to our innate conceptualizations of different actions.[482] To the extent that such strongly held conceptual views exist, it is critical to ensure that we are translating scientific concepts properly so that we know when we are treading on those concepts that we are unable to share as a society.[483]

In short, speaking a common language is a valuable step toward ensuring the proper unfolding of legal analysis.

---

481 *See* Penner, *supra* note 474, at 11–12 (linking the development of first amendment rights to a change in the metaphor describing free speech from a free-flowing river to a marketplace (citing Steven L. Winter, 137 UNIV. OF PA. L. REV. No. 4, 1105, 1188–92)).

482 *See* Penner, *supra* note 474, at 32–33.

483 *Cf.* Penner, *supra* note 474, at 33 (noting that resistance to legal concepts that flow from discordance with our innate conceptualizations should be taken seriously).

Nevertheless, there are surely those who will view the idea of describing science in common language as entirely unrealistic. From this perspective, my comments will fall on the far end of the spectrum, somewhere between dangerous heresy and delightfully appealing myth. For them, I simply note Popper's observation that even myths may contain important truths.[484]

Though language can affect our ability to have a coherent and effective legal conversation, structural elements of the legal system also play in important role. Tribunals that are isolated and insulated are more likely to succumb to troubling temptations. It becomes easier for them to hide behind technical lines and technical terms rather than engaging in the type of hard analysis necessary to grapple with difficult legal dilemmas.

The strongest example of this problem can be found in the tribulations of the modern Federal Circuit. Congress created the Court of Appeals for the Federal Circuit in 1982, designating, among other things, that the court would hear all circuit level patent appeals. The Federal Circuit was intended to bring rationality and uniformity to federal patent appeals on the theory that an appellate group with greater experience in this challenging arena could produce a more coherent body of law.[485] In particular, Congress was concerned

---

484 *See* Popper, *supra* note 300, at 162 (arguing that "historically speaking, all (or nearly all) scientific theories originate from myths, and that a myth may contain important anticipations of scientific theories").

485 *See* Matthew D. Henry & John L. Turner, *The Court of Appeals for the Federal Circuit's Impact on Patent Litigation,* 35 J. LEGAL STUD. 85, 86 (2006); *see also* Fla. Prepaid Postsecondary Educ. Expense Bd. v. College Sav. Bank, 527 U. S. 627, 651 (1999) (Stevens, J., dissenting) (noting that divergence among the federal circuits in their interpretation of patent issues, provided support for the congressional decision in 1982 to consolidate appellate jurisdiction of patent appeals in the Court of Appeals for the Federal Circuit). *See also*

about the inconsistency with which federal appeals courts upheld or overturned the validity of patents.[486]

The Federal Circuit, hailed with such great enthusiasm at the time of its founding, has received unrelenting criticism in the subsequent decades. The Circuit has failed to provide consistency in patent law in general or in the question of patent validity in particular.[487] Most troubling, the Federal Circuit has proven incapable of resolving the disagreements

---

Federal Courts Improvement Act of 1982, 97 P.L. Sec. 125, 97th Cong. (1982) (establishing that the "United States Court of Appeals for the Federal Circuit shall have exclusive jurisdiction . . . (2) of an appeal from a judgment in a civil action for patent infringement").

486 *See* Henry & Turner, *supra* note 482.

487 *See, e.g.*, Kimberly A. Moore, *Markman Eight Years Later: Is Claim Construction More Predictable?*, 9 LEWIS & CLARK L. REV. 231, 231–333 (2005) (documenting a concern among the bench and bar that the Federal Circuit's de novo review of district court claim construction decisions and lack of guidance have caused considerable unpredictability); Joseph Scott Miller, *Enhancing Patent Disclosure for Faithful Claim Construction*, 9 LEWIS & CLARK L. REV. 177, 177 (2005) (arguing that claim construction jurisprudence is in disarray and noting that the Federal Circuit reverses trial court claim construction decisions at a worryingly high rate); *see also* R. Polk Wagner and Lee Petherbridge, *Is the Federal Circuit Succeeding? An Empirical Assessment of Judicial Performance*, 152 U. PENN. L. REV 1105 (2004); *see also* Jeffrey Lefstin, *The Measure of the Doubt: Dissent, Indeterminacy, and Interpretation at the Federal Circuit*, 58 HASTINGS L.J. 1025, 1027, 1094 (arguing that despite the nearly seamless consensus of problems related to de novo review of patent claim construction, it is the indeterminacy of patent law, rather than the application of patent law by the district courts, or the Federal Circuit's review of the district courts, that is responsible for the current circumstances of patent litigation). *See also* John R. Thomas, *Claim Re-Construction: The Doctrine of Equivalents in the Post-Markman Era,* 87 J. PAT. & TRADEMARK OFF. SOC'Y 781, 793 (2005) (discussing unpredictable judicial claim construction in the Federal Circuit); Donald S. Chisum, *Reforming Patent Law Reform,* 4 J. MARSHALL REV. INTELL. PROP. L. 336, 340 (2005) (discussing claims that the Federal Circuit engages in erratic and unpredictable decision making).

and inconsistencies that arise within the circuit, allowing splits among panels to fester unresolved across decades.

Consider the disarray in Federal Circuit doctrine related to so-called product-by-process claims. As a general matter, patent claims are divided into claims for the product, that is, for a particular item of inventions no matter how it is made, or claims for a process, that is, for a method of doing something. A third category of claims is called product-by-process. In 1991, a Federal Circuit panel ruled in the *Scripps* case that a product-by-process claim would cover not only the product made by the process specified but also the product made in any other manner.[488] The panel decision appeared questionable, in light of earlier case precedent, including an old nineteenth-century Supreme Court decision.[489] One might also argue that the decision appeared questionable in light of the common sense notion of the words "product-by-process," but as noted above, common sense does not always prevail in patent law. In the year after *Scripps*, a different Federal Circuit panel ruled to the contrary that product-by-process claims cover only the product made by the process specified.[490]

488 *See* Scripps Clinic & Research Foundation v. Genentech, Inc., 927 F.2d 1565 (Fed. Cir. 1991).

489 *See* Plummer v. Sargent, 120 U.S. 442, 449 (1887) (holding that "[i]t seems necessarily to follow from this view either that the Tucker patents are void by reason of the anticipation practised by Brocksieper, or that the patented process and product must be restricted to exactly what is described"); *cf. Scripps*, 927 F.2d at 1583 (holding that "[s]ince claims must be construed the same way for validity and for infringement, the correct reading of product-by-process claims is that they are not limited to product prepared by the process set forth in the claims"); *see also* 1 Iver P. Cooper, Biotechnology and the Law § 5B.05[2] (1991).

490 *See* Atlantic Thermoplastics Co, Inc. v. Fytex Corp, 970 F.2d 834 (Fed. Cir. 1992).

The later case was entitled *Atlantic Thermoplastics.* In *Atlantic Thermoplastics*, the panel acknowledged the earlier *Scripps* decision but argued that *Scripps* was not binding on the grounds that "[a] decision that fails to consider Supreme Court precedent does not control if the court determines that the prior panel would have reached a different conclusion if it had considered controlling precedent."[491] In other words, the *Atlantic Thermoplastics* panel argued that if a prior panel decision was precedentially incorrect, later panels were not obliged to follow it.

The issue should have been ripe for consideration of the full Federal Circuit en banc, either on the merits of the definition of a product-by-process claim or on the precedential question of whether a panel of the court is allowed to ignore a prior panel's decision. The Federal Circuit denied en banc nevertheless, prompting an angry dissent from one member of the court that regardless of the merits of the matter, the second panel's action is not only insulting to colleagues on the prior panel. "It is mutiny. It is heresy. It is illegal."[492] The broader court, however, was unmoved.

The Federal Circuit's resistance to precedent is also evident in the doctrine of Patent Misuse and its relationship to antitrust law. Prior to 1986, courts had defined patent misuse as an impermissible attempt to expand the time or scope of the patent.[493] In the 1986 case of *Windsurfing*, however, Chief Judge Markey of the Federal Circuit changed the definition to an impermissible attempt to expand the time or scope of

491 *See id.* at 839 n.2.

492 *See* Atlantic Thermoplastics Co., Inc. v. Faytex Corp., 974 F.2d 1279, 1281 (Fed. Cir. 1992) (Rich, J., dissenting from denial of reh'g *en banc*).

493 For a description of the history of patent misuse as well as the Federal Circuit's modern exploits in this doctrinal area, *see* Feldman, *Insufficiency*, *supra* note 72.

the patent *with anticompetitive effect.*[494] In the *Senza-Gel* opinion nine months later, Judge Markey retreated from his earlier decision, noting in a footnote that though modern economic theory would suggest bringing patent misuse in line with antitrust law, any change would have to await action by the Supreme Court or Congress.[495] In 1988, the Senate tried to do just that, passing a bill that would have prohibited a finding of patent misuse unless the patent holder's actions violated antitrust laws.[496] The language was dropped, however, from the final version of the Act.[497]

Despite these failed efforts, a Federal Circuit panel in the 1992 *Mallincrodt* case returned to the language requiring anticompetitive effect for a finding of patent misuse.[498] The decision cited only the *Windsurfing* case, ignoring its later retraction in *Senza Gel* as well as the failed Congressional effort.[499] Later panels have tried to harmonize *Mallinckrodt* with earlier precedents, leaving a confused doctrine which recites the mantra that patent misuse is a broader wrong than antitrust law while essentially applying antitrust law.[500]

The Federal Circuit's reluctance to resolve disagreements also appears in the written description doctrine.[501] In recent

---

494 *See* Windsurfing Int'l, Inc. v. AMF, Inc., 782 F.2d 995, 1001 (Fed. Cir. 1986) (emphasis added); *see also* Feldman, *Insufficiency*, *supra* note 72, at 418.

495 *See* Senza-Gel Corp. v. Seiffhart, 803 F.2d 661, 665 n.9 (Fed. Cir. 1986).

496 *See* Jere M. Webb & Lawrence A. Locke, *Intellectual Property Misuse: Developments in the Misuse Doctrine,* 4 HARV. J.L. & TECH 257, 264 (citing the Intellectual Property Antitrust Protection Act of 1988, 438 § 201, 100th Cong. § 201) (1988).

497 *See* Kenneth J. Burchfiel, *Patent Misuse and Antitrust Reform: Blessed be the Tie?"*, 4 HARV. J.L. & TECH. 1, 2 n.9 (1991).

498 *See* Mallinckrodt v. Medipart, 976 F.2d 700, 708–09 (Fed. Cir. 1992).

499 *See id.*

500 *See* Feldman, *Insufficiency*, *supra* note 72, at 425–31.

501 For a discussion of the emergence of the written description doctrine and subsequent problems, *see* Feldman, *The Inventor's Contribution*, *supra* note 43;

decades, the Federal Circuit identified within the disclosure doctrines of patent law a separate written description doctrine.[502] The doctrine has caused considerable consternation as courts and litigants have tried to understand the logic for the doctrine as well as the contours of it.[503] In 2002, a government brief noted in a polite understatement that, "[a]lthough this Court has addressed the 'written description' requirement of § 112 on a number of occasions, its decisions have not taken a clear and uniform position regarding the purpose and meaning of the requirement."[504]

The Federal Circuit had an opportunity to address the issue in 2004 in an en banc petition for the case of *Rochester v. Searle*, which had applied the written description doctrine. The court refused to take the case en banc, and the denial produced five separate dissenting and concurring opinions arguing over whether the doctrine should exist and what its contours should be.[505]

---

see also Paula K. Davis, *Questioning the Requirement for Written Description: Enzo Biochem v. Gen-Probe and Overly Broad Patent Cases*, 37 IND. L. REV. 467, 500 (2004); Cynthia M. Lambert, *Gentry Gallery and the Written Description Requirement,* 7 B.U. J. SCI. & TECH. L. 109, 139 (2001); Daniel P. Chisholm, *The Effect of the USPTO's Written Description Guidelines on Gene Patent Applications,* 35 SUFFOLK U. L. REV. 543, 570 (2001).

502 *See* Regents of the Univ. of Cal. v. Eli Lilly & Co., 119 F.3d 1559 (Fed. Cir. 1997).

503 *See e.g.,* Univ. of Rochester v. G.D. Searle & Co., 375 F.3d 1303, 1314 (Fed. Cir. 2004) (denial of reh'g *en banc*) (Rader, J., dissenting) (listing 7 law review articles defending the *Eli Lilly* written description requirement, 31 criticizing the requirement, and 16 giving the holding neutral treatment as illustration of the confusion generated by the decision).

504 *See id.* at 1309 (citing brief of amicus curiae at 4–5 requesting en banc consideration in Enzo Biochem, Inc. v. Gen-Probe Inc., 323 F.3d 956 (Fed. Cir. 2002)).

505 *See* Univ. of Rochester v. G.D. Searle 7 Co., 375 F.3d 1303 (Fed. Cir. 2004) (denial of reh'g *en banc*).

Problems in the Federal Circuit are not surprising. In fact, they are structurally predictable. The Federal Circuit cannot benefit from the balancing effects that may occur with multicircuit consideration of the same issues. While any isolated court is at risk, a court with a primary focus on scientific cases is particularly vulnerable. Courts can easily lose themselves in the technical aspects of the cases, which provide camouflage for the failure to resolve issues or to resolve them in a rational manner. In addition, the parties tend to shroud themselves in jargon which can obscure the issues at hand for both the Federal Circuit and for the Supreme Court justices who might consider wading into the issues.

Supervision can ameliorate the problems of isolation, but the amount of energy the Supreme Court can devote to one circuit is limited. Although the Court has recently begun to accept a number of appeals from the Federal Circuit, it has taken decades for the Court to engage extensively with Federal Circuit doctrines,[506] and the Supreme Court cannot single handedly compensate for the structural inadequacies of the Federal Circuit design. In short, courts that

---

506 *See* Gregory A. Castanias et al, *A Review of Recent Decisions of the Federal Circuit Court*, 56 AM. U.L. REV. 793, 798 (2007) (citing commentary in the mid-1990s, which concluded that the Supreme Court rarely took cases from the Federal Circuits and exhibited more even more deference to the Federal Circuit on substantive **patent** law issues than on other substantive law issues, and comparing that to the current wave of Supreme Court interest in Federal Circuit cases in general and patent cases in particular); *see also* Address of Chief Judge Paul R. Michel to the Federal Circuit Judicial Conference on the State of the Court, Grand Hyatt Washington, D.C., May 15, 2008 (noting that the Supreme Court grants certiorari in roughly one percent of the petitions filed, with a slightly higher rate of acceptance for petitions arising out of the Federal Circuit).

must engage in scientific analysis should be integrated, not isolated.

The need to encourage a common language of communication and our experiences with the Federal Circuit should cast doubt on recent legislative proposals such as a recent bill to create separate intellectual property courts[507] and a bill to allow district court judges to defer patent cases to colleagues considered better-versed in patent law.[508] These legislative proposals echo other calls in recent years to create specialized tribunals including drug courts, community courts, mental health courts, and domestic violence courts.[509]

Such moves are likely to fuel the temptation to obscure difficult issues in a blaze of technical terms. The goal should be to encourage translation of scientific terms into understandable concepts, rather than to indulge jargon by creating its own forum.

---

507 H.R. 5418, 109th Cong. (as passed by the House, September 28, 2006); *see also Special IP Trial Courts A Bad Idea, Lawyers Say*, IP LAW 360, Feb. 1, 2006, http://ip.law360.com/Members/ViewArticlePortion.aspx?Id=5183&ReturnUrl=..%2fsecure%2fViewArticle.aspx%3fId%3d5183; *but see also* Lefstin, *supra* note 470, at 1047 (arguing that specialized trial courts would undoubtedly improve patent litigation); Kimberly A. Moore, *Forum Shopping in Patent Cases: Does Geographic Choice Affect Innovation?*, 77 N. CAROL. L. REV. 889, 932–34 (2001) (arguing in favor of specialized patent trial courts in order to deter forum shopping). The bill passed the House in 2007 but died in the Senate. Lawrence M. Sung, *Strangers in a Strange Land: Specialized Courts Resolving Patent Disputes*, BUSINESS LAW TODAY, Mar.–Apr. 2008, at 28.

508 Anne Broache, *House OKs Specialized Patent Judges,* CNET NEWS.COM, (Feb. 13, 2007), http://news.com.com/2061-10796_3-6158928.html?part=rss&tag=2327-10784-0&subj=news&tag=cnetfd.blog.

509 Sung, *supra* note 504, at 27.

D. THE EMBRACE OF IMPERFECTION

The sections above have explored the inclination to reach for science in an effort to solve law's difficult dilemmas. The powerful allure of science flows in part from our distress over the weakness and imperfection of law. It is tempting to see law as a hopeless enterprise, distorted by biased perceptions, hampered by ineptitude, and cluttered with contradictions.

Moreover, certain crosscurrents in modern legal theory may make us particularly susceptible to the call of science. I do not mean to suggest that there is something unique about today. The same theme emerges repeatedly throughout hundreds of years of legal history. Nevertheless, this moment may be ripe for more of the same, and it offers an opportunity for reflection rather than a reflexive response.

Our vision of the appeal of science flows both from a sense that science is transformative and from a sense that science is accessible to all, including the humble lawyer. Science is transforming our lives at a remarkably rapid pace. Many of those who inhabit the halls of legal academia can remember when the day-to-day working life did not include even voicemail or email, let alone the vast networking and researching power of the Internet and the range of small devices that put all of that power in a hand-held, portable form. The pace of medical science and biology has been no less breathtaking. Life-saving biotech drugs, genetically engineered crops, and medical research based on genetic engineering have exploded in the last twenty-five years. As described above, imaging techniques, which tell us what parts of the brain are active when a subject is engaged in various tasks, give researchers a window into the human brain when it is alive, well and active and allow us to hypothesize about what legal incentives may drive or affect human behavior.

All of this science feels somehow within our reach, a tool that we can use, even if we do not fully grasp it. Computers make everyone an armchair empiricist. Easy Internet access to scientific journals and articles gives the impression of an ability to reach for scientific data with ease, regardless of whether we actually understand its assumptions and limitations.

In contrast to our view that science is transformative and within our reach, law appears damaged and weak. There are no emerging legal theories that offer hope for galvanizing our faith in the law. Moreover, the criticisms that various schools of thought have brought to bear on the process of law seem to expose flaws that reach down to its structural integrity.[510] Anything deconstructed loses power, although ultimately, the instinct to deconstruct everything loses power, itself, by leaving nothing. Nevertheless, with these critical perspectives in mind, the siren song of science is particularly strong. It tempts us to abandon the effort to find clarity and meaning in law and to abdicate to a realm that appears to offer structure and coherence. We reach for science in our never-ending quest for certainty. Lessening the desire for legal perfection, however, could soften the instinct to abdicate to science.

I do not share the despair of those who find hopelessness in the law's lack of perfection or who see chaos as the central feature of law. Law will never have the elegant truth and exquisite objectivity of a mathematical formula or even the more limited reliability of a biological theory. Law is messy, full of missteps, and the ground beneath it is constantly

---

510 *Cf.* Merton, *supra* note 446, at 264 (arguing that although logically, to establish the empirical genesis of beliefs and values is not to deny their validity, this is often the psychological effect).

shifting as new cases arise and additional legislation appears. It is an imperfect process of evolution and adaptation to constantly changing circumstances. Nevertheless, it is critical to understand that science itself lacks the capacity to answer the questions that law must address.

Law is not a process that can be replaced by science. It should be embraced for what it is, rather than neutered in an attempt to make it something else. Law must be celebrated on its own terms, in all its glory and imperfection.

CHAPTER IX

Conclusion

The law professor Stephen Goldberg relates a wonderful series of anecdotes about the modern image of lawyers and scientists.[511] Over the years, he has asked law students to name the most brilliant person who ever lived. Scientists predominate, with Einstein and Newton topping the charts. Mozart and Shakespeare enter as well, with occasional votes for Plato and Freud. Goldberg notes that he has "asked the same question of scientists, musicians, and others, and the result is always the same. No one ever names a lawyer."[512] His experience reflects the images of law and science that lead us to keep latching onto science to solve our problems.

Law's love affair with science can be traced through hundreds of years of legal history. It takes the form both of

511 *See* Stephen Goldberg, *The Reluctant Embrace: Law and Science in America,* 75 Geo. L.J. 1341, 1341 (1987).

512 *See id.* at 1341.

attempts to import science into law and of attempts to export law's problems to the experts of science. Even when we do not go quite so far as import or export, we all too frequently wrap ourselves in scientific jargon, as if simply adapting the language of science will endow our decisions with wisdom and elegance. Throughout this history, it is remarkable how often we turn to science to soothe concerns over the inadequacies and imperfections of law.

Our perpetual forays to find better law through science are incapable of solving law's frustrations, but they do create distortions in the legal realm. When the legal system relies on science for crafting rules, those rules lack the flexibility and dexterity necessary for effective participation in the process of legal evolution. Moreover, relying on science creates the illusion of reasonable resolution. It masks our failure to resolve the issues at hand or to take responsibility for the decisions we have made. We gain authority through obscurity, rather than earning it through the careful unfolding of legal analysis. We pay the price with unresolved issues and doctrines that are not susceptible to the process of interpretation and adaptation that is so essential to law.

We are unlikely to escape the cycle of exaltation and disappointment unless we are willing to abandon our misguided yearning for completion and perfection in law. If, however, we can adjust our vision of both law and science, we may be able to recognize that law has no need of rescue and that science can never be a knight in shining armor. Law's answers, as imperfect as they are, must be developed within law itself.

Table of Cases

E

F

G

Index

D